FROM HELL
to
Happiness

HOW TO HEAL WHEN YOUR
LOVED ONE IS TERMINAL

CHRISTOPHER COOPER

In loving memory of my late wife, Jennifer Kay Cooper.

"You cannot alter your fate; however, you can rise to meet it."

- HII-SAMA, *PRINCESS MONONOKE*

Contents

Foreword

The day I met Chris, before he came in for his first appointment, my assistant Hailey briefed me on the situation. As a human being, I was distressed by the unbelievably sad story I was hearing. As a counselor, I was intimidated. My job is typically to give people hope that things can and will get better, but I kept questioning, how am I going to help this man whose wife is dying, find hope that things will get better? They won't. She is going to die. His children will grow up without their mom. When he came in, I immediately realized he was young – too young to be going through this. He was only thirty years old. This is important to note because most books that are written on this topic discuss an older generation of people and the hardships they encounter. Usually, the people struck by terminal illness have already completed a career, raised their children and are in their retirement years. This book brings a new dynamic. To be so young and have your whole life ahead of you, only to find out you or a younger loved one is terminal, brings about an entirely new set of challenges. He was timid and somewhat reserved. I could see that it was difficult for him to open up and talk. Honestly, I didn't know where to begin, but I gently began asking questions and eased into a conversation with him. In talking with him, I could clearly see a man who didn't believe in being a victim to his circumstances. If there was a way to get through this and come out the other side as a healthy individual, he intended to do it. Actually, it seemed that for him, there was no other option. Based on the type of person he seemed to be, I began to put my plan together. There are 5 stages of grief, the last one being acceptance. I decided to start with the end in mind – acceptance. We would face this ugly reality head on. We would not let it take away the very best parts of him or his children, for if we did, her death would be in vain. We would find a way to get him and his babies through this and find happiness again.

In Chris' situation, knowing he had no way out and was looking to me for support, I could only do one thing and that was to guide him through each stage of grief by helping him find acceptance of where he was, emotionally.

In the case of a terminally ill loved one, grief starts before the death and often times, at the moment one is diagnosed as terminal. The five stages of grief are well documented and in fact, there is an amazing book that will guide someone through the entire process. It is, "On Grief and Grieving: Finding the Meaning of Grief Through the Five Stages of Loss" by Elisabeth Kübler-Ross.

Acceptance of Denial – Denial is usually the first stage that we experience when we begin to grieve. We feel overwhelmed and can't make sense of what has just happened. We will say things like, "I can't believe this is happening." Denial is a protective mechanism used by the brain to keep us from "losing it." In the beginning, it is a quite effective and healthy tool to utilize so that we can function. Learning to use the tool for our benefit and not fighting it is important. This is acceptance of denial.

Acceptance of Bargaining – Bargaining is characterized by, well, bargaining. This can look like, "If you let my wife live, I will never doubt you again, God." Or, "What if we had quit smoking sooner? Maybe she wouldn't be dying." It is quite natural for your brain to try and make sense of the tragedy. We are taught that everything happens for a reason, so one of the first things we do is look for a reason. Even though, logically, we know that no amount of "what-if's" will change our situation, it is important for us to find a "reason" because it helps us begin to function again. Allow yourself to bargain as much as you need to in order to find some order in your universe again. This is acceptance of bargaining.

Acceptance of Anger – Anger is self-explanatory. However, we often begin to feel a sense of guilt because we "shouldn't" be angry. Sometimes we are even angry with the loved one who is dying. If we didn't have anger as one of our many emotions, we would feel such an immense sadness that it would consume us. So in this respect, anger is also healthy. Allow yourself to feel the anger completely. Vent. Find a safe way to release it. Do not fight it. Do not allow yourself to feel guilty for feeling it. This is acceptance of anger.

Acceptance of Depression – Once we have found our way through denial, bargaining and anger, we begin to move into a depression. We are tired. All of our efforts to pretend this isn't happening, find a reason why it's happening and get pissed off because it is happening hasn't stopped it from happening. Then we break. We cry, we isolate, we feel hopeless. This is a necessary step in grieving because from this point, we can begin to release control over the situation. Releasing control over the situation allows us to move towards acceptance and the final phase of our grief. Accept the depression. It's temporary. Things will get better.

Acceptance of Acceptance – When we finally begin to accept that this is our new "new" in life, we will often try to fight it.

We, again, try to find guilt in this. We believe that accepting this new fate means that it is "OK" that it happened. This is not what acceptance is. Acceptance is just beginning to adjust to the new life without our loved one. Allow yourself to accept the death and begin to function again. This is acceptance of acceptance.

Chris describes his intimate knowledge of the stages in his book and when he came in for therapy, he would always ask me, "Is it okay that I feel like this?" I, of course, said yes. Absolutely. In fact, you must feel every minute of this emotion. Allow it to come. Allow it to envelop you. The more that you allow it, the sooner it will pass. The opposite is also true. The more you fight it, the longer it will take. Be kind to yourself. Be gentle with yourself. You are only a human.

There was one more specific stage that Chris would go through and I knew it. As soon as the devastation of his wife dying actually became real to him, I knew it would be difficult for him to carry on as normal; however, he had to. He had two small children who had just lost their mother and would desperately need structure and order, as well as the loving arms of a father. He had to be there for them. Dissociation often looks like denial but is a little different. Dissociation is a sense of being cut off from the real world, like you're in a daze. Because I knew he would enter this stage, we decided to begin setting routines in place that would serve as an "auto-pilot." He would be very structured with family routines and would learn to cook certain meals while Jenn was still alive. Chris didn't need to learn to cook for the children and figure out a nightly routine or a morning routine after Jenn died, as it would be overwhelming. So, we circumvented the dissociation and used this to our advantage. By the time that Jenn passed, Chris was in a habitual routine that served to get him and the children through until he could come out of the fog.

While Chris doesn't claim to be a man of faith, I saw enough faith in him to move mountains. From day one, he was determined to bring himself and his children through this life-altering tragedy. He has done the impossible, the unthinkable. He and his children have endured one of the most painful tragedies that humans can encounter. They are not only alive, but they are thriving. Yes, they miss Jenn. How could they not? But they have adjusted and accepted this new life to the fullest potential. This could have turned out so differently had it not been for Chris' unyielding faith and determination. In reading the book, I found it wonderfully refreshing. Not having gone through this myself, I was still able to relate to the emotions and grief, as well as understand how I might use the techniques in other situations in my life. Most self-help books are lists of dos and don'ts, but not Chris'. He found a way to narrate his story in a fashion that lends to easy reading and an understanding of how one might get through this themselves, without all of the lists and note keeping that might generally be needed.

Misty Locknane, BS, LCDC, CCS, CART

Owner/The Alpha Center

Prologue

Breaking Point

"Ask for help, not because you're weak, but because you want to remain strong."

– LES BROWN

"THAT... WAS THE worst pain I have ever felt in my entire life," my wife said in tears. "I really thought I was going to die. I never want to go through that pain again!" She looked up at me, still clutching her stomach after a long and intense spasm, the first of many she would end up having. "And I know it's just going to get worse! I don't want to go through that ever again!" She paused. I didn't know what to say. "If it happens again, if something happens to me, like... if I stop breathing or go into shock, I want you to just let me go. Don't try to bring me back. Just let me die."

My heart, which was already ripping at the seams, tore apart. I knew instantly that as her husband, who had faithfully walked hand in hand with her through this hell of her cancer journey, I had to support whatever decision she made. To do otherwise would be a betrayal. But I was in shock. As if our situation hadn't been real enough for me in the past year and a half, suddenly comprehending that these diaphragm tumors could trigger her imminent death, broke me in a way I had not yet experienced. So I pleaded.

"You would rather die than go through that again?"

She looked at me through tears. Her black hair had long since been taken by the chemotherapy treatments. She felt like a disgusting monster. First, the steroids had caused her to regain the weight she had worked so hard to take off, then her skin-sparing double mastectomy, which left her flat-chested save some bunched-up skin, gave her a bowling pin shaped torso. Nothing I could do or say would rescue her self-image. She had constant, persistent pain in numerous places throughout her body. She always did her best not to complain around the boys or other people, but among myself and her inner circle, she let it all out.

After more than a year and a half of fighting, thinking we had beat her cancer, and then finding out it was back for good, that it would eventually kill her, after her struggling through countless rounds of treatment and the horrible side effects it caused, after all of that, she was exhausted. Jenn didn't want to die, but she was ready. This spasm, which she described as exponentially more painful than child labor contractions, and which must have lasted for twenty minutes as we lay on the living room floor, she curled in the fetal position while I held and talked her through it, this was the thing that finally broke her.

"Chris, I have done everything I can to give you and the boys as much time as I can. But I'm tired. And that pain," her voice started to break again, "was the worst pain of my entire life! I'm scared! I don't want to ever go through that again! So yes, and

I'm sorry, but if it happens again and there's a chance I can die and not have to go through it again, then just let me die!"

I broke, fully and completely. Of course, I agreed, but I felt what little of myself had remained intact shatter into pieces, joining the rest of the pieces that had already fallen. After we finished that unpleasant conversation she retreated to the bedroom. I stayed behind to process the gravity of where we were now. I cried, then there would be a reprieve, followed by more crying. At some point I realized I had moved from the couch to the floor, and there I found myself, in a heap, letting the pain out as best I knew how.

For eighteen months I had managed to keep it together without needing therapy or medication, though I did call friends occasionally. I put on a brave front, but often cried uncontrollably in the car by myself, or while in the bath. The coping mechanisms I had developed to get by, if barely, failed. Whatever strength remained in the weakened grip on my mental health finally gave out. I felt it. I had been depressed before, to the point that I let go of all my responsibilities. I was younger then, with no family to take care of. But now, without getting help, where would we be? My back was against the wall.

I crawled to the couch and leveraged it to get on my feet. My dad had left me a business card of a therapist, who previously helped him. Therapy was not foreign to me. I saw someone, as a young teenager, after moving in with my dad, and it changed my life. Scheduling appointments with this therapist, and asking my regular doctor about antidepressants, had been on my to-do list for months. I knew I needed help, but lacked the motivation to do something about it. Not that I had a lot of spare time as a full-time teacher. Now I decided to just call.

Even though business hours were over, I would at least be able to leave a voicemail.

I walked to the desk in my bedroom and opened the drawer under the keyboard. It was full of disorganized papers, cards and writing utensils. I scrambled through the mess to find the card of the woman who would guide me down the path of putting my life back together one fragment at a time. At least I felt grateful that my in-laws had the boys. By now, they understood Jenn's cancer was slowly killing her. How terrified would they have been had they witnessed their mother writhing in pain on the living room floor? I dialed the number hoping someone might answer despite the late hour, even though I had no idea what to say.

A woman's soothing voice answered, "You've reached the Alpha Center. If this is an emergency, hang up and dial nine one one. Our normal business hours..." In a way I was relieved I would not have to break down in front of a live person. Waiting for the tone, I still did not know what to say.

"Hello... My name is Chris Cooper. My wife is dying from cancer..." I felt my throat tighten, but fought through it. "I need help. Please. If you have any openings, I really need some help." I was begging, on my knees once again. "I can't do this by myself anymore. Please, help me. If you have any appointments, my phone number is... Thank you."

Hanging up the phone, I felt a small sense of relief. I had finally taken the first step to help myself. If I was lucky, they'd have an opening, and I'd get a call back. This ended up being the start of my long recovery. That night was one of the worst moments in my hell, and that phone call was the first of many tiny steps out of it.

Please understand I am not a professional counselor or therapist. My Texas All-Level Teaching for Music certification involves a lot of life coaching but has absolutely nothing to do with grief counseling. I am just a guy who has gone through the horrific experience of slowly losing his wife and the mother of his children to a terminal illness over the course of two years and nine months. I am simply a man who did not cheat nor abandon his sick wife – which unfortunately does happen to many women with breast cancer. I fulfilled my marital vows fully and to the end: "until death do us part."

By sharing my story in this book, I hope to help others who are going through their own devastation or grief. Cancer sucks. Any terminal illness sucks. You watch your loved one disappear one small piece at a time. Sometimes it takes a while before you realize, "Wow, they didn't used to be this way." It is hard. It is gut wrenching. How do you cope when the life you built with someone you love is falling apart?

I offer no promises or easy answers. These pages do not contain expert opinions or science but my personal experience. You may learn more about your own journey by reading about mine. While everyone's grieving process is different, many of the emotions and coping mechanisms are the same. What worked for me and my family might work for you and yours.

I truly hope something in this book eases your way through hell and back to happiness, and lets you once again find the light in your life.

Chapter 1

From Happiness

"I miss me. The old me, the happy me, the bright me, the smiling me, the laughing me, the gone me."

– AUTHOR UNKONWN

L IFE BEFORE CANCER was so good. We were living the dream. I think heaven and hell exist in our reality, each a state of mind. Before cancer, we lived in our personal heaven. I miss the life Jenn and I built together, the life my boys and I will never recover.

I had turned twenty-one a few months before meeting Jenn. It was December of my second year at Angelo State University in San Angelo, Texas and I worked at a call center as a customer service representative for a major credit card company. Jenn had worked there for much longer, but we had never crossed paths, because she typically worked the overnight shift. That is until a reduction in those positions forced her into the lower paying evening shift.

One night I was answering calls, while she was sitting in the next cubicle. She had broken up with a jerk boyfriend, and was venting to a co-worker about how she was going to date someone older than her next time. She listed several other requirements, too, none of which I met, except I was at least old enough to buy her a drink. You overhear chitchat all the time in a place like that. I didn't think much of it, and soon I was busy on another call.

Jenn saw my reflection in the window while I wasn't paying attention to her, and thought I was cute. She started talking to me, but I've always been slow to pick up on cues from women.

Then she found me on MySpace. Remember that site? It felt creepy, to be honest. How did she know my last name? How did she find me? The only information I had given her was my first name. I heard Twilight Zone music in my head as I read a message from her.

The next day she handed me a pay stub I had forgotten to take home. That's how she found my last name. I felt silly, and after that we chatted a lot and ended up hanging out.

One night we went to IHOP after work. She brought along a friend and mutual co-worker to help make the evening less awkward. We had a great time, but then our co-worker had to leave. I wondered, would she stay or use that as her excuse to end our evening, too? She stayed, and I thought, "Okay, here we go!" We did hit it off very quickly and spent another couple of hours talking about music. We shared a common background, both being only children and personal challenges we had faced growing up, including coping with alcoholism in our families.

I can't remember how long it took me to ask her out. She gave me all the signs and then some. She made a CD with tracks from the band Bayside to introduce me to them, and I loved it.

We would talk on the phone for over an hour every night. One day she said, "I think I might be getting a crush on you!"

I wasn't ready to date yet, so I responded with, "That would be okay."

I had broken up with someone recently. For two months I had worked on myself, figuring out how to become a better person and be happy on my own. Though I felt better, I didn't know if I was ready for another long-term relationship. Most of my relationships had lasted over a year, so was a two-month break enough for me to do all of that again? That's why I was hesitant.

At some point she told me: "If you ask me out, I'll say yes. But no pressure." I couldn't keep her waiting forever. It took about two weeks from the time we first talked until I invited her to go out, and even then I only got the confidence to jump into it with the help of friends. But once we started dating, I fell fast and hard.

It felt like being caught in a whirlwind, the same as in the movies. Within two weeks, I knew I wanted to marry Jenn. I proposed to her after six months of dating, and we were married three months later. Everything moved extremely fast. It was just like you read in fairy tales.

When I met Jenn, I was trying to decide what to do with my life and what kind of college degree to pursue. I had washed out of the Music Department at West Texas A & M University during my first depression, which I refer to as the "Bad Old Days." After that, I believed I wasn't responsible enough to be a music major, but friends in my band and a few professors at my new school thought I should pursue music if that's what I wanted. Still, I was debating between Communications and Music.

For two years I was officially an undecided student. The day we learned Jenn was pregnant, something incredible happened. We took her mom to Chili's to celebrate. Jenn's biggest dream in life had been having children, being a stay-at-home wife and mother. Unfortunately she was unable to get pregnant in her previous marriage, which left her feeling broken and devastated. So now, even though Jenn and I were not married, the sheer joy of the pregnancy crushed any concerns she or her mom might have had regarding my intentions.

During the meal I suddenly realized I needed to decide what I wanted to do with my life. I should hurry up and finish college, so I could start providing for Jenn and our unborn child. I said as much out loud.

"Well, we don't want you to drop out. We want you to be happy and do what you want to do," Jenn and her mom agreed. Then Jenn asked, "So, what do you want to do?"

Without hesitation, I said, "I want to be a band director." It was amazing. All my doubts had vanished, and I knew the right path for me.

We made a plan to achieve our dream life. Jenn agreed to move into my apartment so I could care for her during the pregnancy. Even though Jenn desired to stay home with the baby, she would continue working while I went to college, so I could focus on my studies and still have time for our family. In return, I would work extremely hard as a Music Major, and once I became Band Director, she could stop working and be a stay-at-home mom and wife.

I wanted to propose immediately, but could not afford a ring. A dear friend of the family offered a diamond band that had been passed down from her mom. We made a five hour road trip to Austin to visit, and retrieve the ring. Since Jenn was with me and knew it was coming, I proposed in our hotel room. I promised myself to make up for this rather unromantic approach on a later anniversary celebration.

Jenn and I got along so well. We had been living together for six months before the wedding, and I had not detected a single red flag, much less a deal breaker.

Jenn's pregnancy was wonderful. She was radiant and elated, any discomfort insignificant in light of becoming a mother. None of the horror stories I heard about pregnant women applied to Jenn.

Our wedding day was perfect. We spent quality time with a huge crowd of family and friends at a lake house before saying our vows at sunset. Afterward, we had a reception and danced until late into the night.

Jenn and I on our wedding day.

I was terrified about being a father. The doctors told us we were having a girl, but Jenn felt certain it was going to be a boy. We had two names picked out just in case. Not for the first time, Jenn was correct in her prediction about the future. The day she gave birth to our son Devin was one of the best days of my life.

After Devin was born, everything changed, which presented significant challenges during our first two years of marriage. Some of it was my fault, but Jenn had some serious issues to work out.

Jenn was my first wife, but I was her second husband. Her first husband had treated her terribly. They married soon after graduating high school, and she followed him to the United

Kingdom where he was deployed as a member of the United States Air Force.

She became isolated and lonely. It got worse when her husband chose to hang out with friends after work rather than coming home. Eventually, he cheated on her. Jenn became so depressed that she began drinking alcohol and eating too much. Her body changed from model figure to morbidly obese. One night she took a few fists full of pills and ended up paralyzed on the bathroom floor. When her husband got back home, he saw her on the floor, pills scattered everywhere, and declared, "I just can't do this right now." Instead of calling an ambulance, he went to bed.

There was physical abuse as well. He would force Jenn to perform oral sex, continuing despite her frequent tears. All of this had profound ramifications on her sense of self-worth.

The male figures throughout her life had been flawed, beginning with her father leaving when she was still a baby. After years of silence he returned when Jenn was a young adult, explaining his failings with addiction struggles and a false sense of belief that she would be better off without him. Thankfully, they were able to repair some of the damage and had a good relationship by the time he passed away.

Every boyfriend had been possessive, abusive and unfaithful. You can imagine the toll this took on her self-esteem.

I didn't see any of these effects while we were dating. Jenn seemed humble, aware of imperfections and eager to improve herself. I share that ideal, and thought it made us more compatible.

To my bewilderment, all her built up insecurities came out right after Devin was born. I strive to be a good guy, be affectionate and make romantic gestures to show my appreciation and love. I was treating her the same way I always had, but suddenly that was not enough anymore.

My mistake was not devoting enough time to Jenn and Devin. Between work, officer duties for my band fraternity, collegiate studies and other band activities, I had to find a balance. Things remained rough, despite the sacrifices I made in my efforts to be a better husband and father. Jenn also suffered from postpartum depression, which amplified her insecurities and caused her to lash out at me. The woman I married had disappeared.

It did not help that we stayed in a tiny trailer next to my mother-in-law's house for the first year of Devin's life. We had moved out of my apartment and into this office trailer, to save money for Devin's arrival. We never intended to still be there after his birth, but we just weren't able to save as much as we had planned. With only a mini fridge and microwave, we spent a lot on fast food. Cigarettes and debts kept us strapped for cash. We both gained weight from the constant eating out. There was a working toilet, but we had to go to her mom's house to shower. The trailer was so narrow there was barely a path between the entertainment center and the couch. I would sit on the couch and put my feet up on the entertainment center's lower shelf. I am glad Devin was just a baby, so he does not remember how bad that place was.

Devin, about one year old.

We both hated the trailer, and once we could finally afford to get into an apartment, life improved significantly. Until I started getting healthier.

One day I was bringing Devin home from daycare. We lived in a second floor apartment, and as I was climbing the steps, I noticed how laborious it felt. When I reached the top, I was incredibly winded from carrying my backpack up one flight of stairs. I said to myself, "Screw this. I'm tired of being overweight and out of shape. I can't even climb the stairs without being winded. I'm going to change. I want to be healthy again!"

It was mid-December, so I set a date for New Year's Day and began researching. I crafted an achievable meal plan and decided my approach to exercise. I started out with a few simple body weight exercises and a twenty minute walk/jog.

Jenn helped my efforts by learning how to prepare healthier meals. Eight months later I had lost about eighty-five pounds.

Once I looked trim and muscular, Jenn began to worry. She saw me as this great, handsome guy, in college, surrounded by cute girls interested in the band, while she was more into choir/theater. Our sex life had not been great, mostly because she felt insecure about her looks, so why would I *not* cheat on her? Especially when every other guy before me had.

Being accused of cheating made me sad and angry. Despite all our challenges, I had always remained faithful to her. Most infuriating was that proving your innocence is impossible. She either had to believe me or not.

It shook me to the core. I had always prided myself on having positive, healthy relationships, but I was out of ideas. If Jenn thought I was cheating, divorce could be right around the corner.

Whenever I need help with anything – I research it. I bought a book called *The Love Dare* by Alex and Stephen Kendrick, which is a study on marriage from the Christian perspective and includes a series of forty daily challenges to turn even the worst marriage around. Online I found a wonderful resource called *Marriage Builders*. All their material was free, so I printed it – over two thousand pages – and began reading and analyzing my marriage.

The daily challenges were tough. After her constant accusations, I had inadvertently retaliated by taking verbal jabs at her. I had to stop doing that. One challenge said to do something romantic, so I bought her cheap flowers – we were broke – and took them to her work. She loved it. Later, I let Devin bring the flowers. Jenn's co-workers were quite jealous of this weekly tradition, which I maintained for several months. I also started helping more around the house and in general. It was tough, because she wasn't treating me any better for a while. I was busting my ass to save our marriage, and all I received in return were complaints about my shortcomings, the apartment – which was the best we could afford at the time – and accusations of cheating.

Thankfully, all my hard work paid off in the end. Slowly, Jenn realized how much she meant to me. She took notice of the extreme efforts I had made to improve our marriage, and trusted me more. After a while, she began to reciprocate my feelings and affections. We were heading in the right direction.

For our second wedding anniversary, I wanted to do something extraordinary, to make her feel special. A scavenger hunt crossed my mind and I immediately got to work.

Meanwhile, Jenn had seen a daytime television talk show, about wives in their second or third marriages, who were unintentionally punishing their current husbands for the wrongdoings of their previous spouses. She realized she had been doing the exact same thing to me.

The day of our second wedding anniversary arrived. Every detail was meticulously planned and executed. Jenn came home from work and found a "golden ticket". I tried to make it look as close to the golden ticket from the old *Willy Wonka* movie as possible. She was given a clue and instructions to let me know when she left the house. She also received a CD to put in her car stereo.

Jenn set off on her adventure. The first track on the Scavenger Hunt Soundtrack was from the *Willy Wonka* movie, Uncle Joe singing, *I've Got a Golden Ticket*. I could practically feel her smile and excitement. The remaining songs we had dedicated to each other over the previous two years. She was guided to the restaurant where we had our first date. There, they handed her four roses along with the next clue – how cool were they to do that for me? This took her to the location of our first anniversary dinner, next to the San Angelo Riverwalk. She found four more roses and a clue that directed her back home. My master plan was working.

At our house she found a note instructing her to enjoy a bath I had prepared. The tub was hot with bubbles, bath salts, a glass of wine, and candles illuminating the dark. I had more music prepared. Slow jams and other relaxing, romantic music, meaningful to us. I had asked her to let me know when she was ready to get out, so I could hand her a warm towel. But, I screwed that part up. Turns out, putting a towel in the microwave will burn a hole in it.

I had left a note for Jenn to put on her sexiest dress and meet me in the living room. In the meantime, I had put on my suit and was waiting with the candle light dinner I had prepared...ok, ordered from our favorite restaurant. But I had done the plating and decorations, playing a third CD filled with jazzy, classic music such as Frank Sinatra. Her bold choice for a dress not only took my breath away, but felt like a major victory, because it was a clear signal that I had finally won her over again. It was perfect.

The last surprise came after dinner, I had moved the table out of the way and selected our wedding song. Then I asked, "May I have this dance?" and she happily accepted.

It was an incredibly rewarding evening. The most romantic plan I ever pulled off. I'm not sure I'll be able to top that.

Jenn later explained how she had been unintentionally punishing me for what her first husband had done, and that she was committed to change. She promised to accept my love with an open heart and trust me completely. Our marriage only got stronger from that day forward.

We moved to Eden, Texas, for my first teaching job. Jenn had been pregnant again. Our second son, Kayden, was born in early August, only a couple of weeks before school started and while I was running a summer camp for my first band program. He was a real handful. As a baby, Devin slept at odd hours, but for long stretches. Kayden despised sleeping. Devin was four years old at the time, and loved holding his little brother. There is something magical about the ages between three and seven, when children are at their most adorable.

Devin was still my little buddy and a happy kid. Kayden was either quiet or throwing a fit, and never slept. We took turns rocking him, singing to him for two hours or more each night to help him fall asleep. Despite the exhaustion, we adored Kayden, and were amazed by each new thing he learned to do. After a rough first year, he became just as happy as Devin.

I was passionate about my work, teaching music to grades one through four, fifth and sixth grade band, and a grade seven through twelve high school band. Everything was new, and despite not being quite ready to run my own program, I enjoyed making all the decisions. My first marching band contest was a disaster, but I learned a lot, fixed what I needed to, and over time the kids improved dramatically. The Christmas Concert was a huge hit in town, and the band received top ratings for their performances at the University Interscholastic League Concert Contest and for another festival at the Myerson Symphony Center in Dallas, Texas. It is one of the most beautiful and historic performance halls in Texas. The acoustics are phenomenal. These accomplishments were a turning point and the band went from being a local joke to a great source of pride for the town. One of our songs even advanced to the second round of a recording based contest called the ATSSB Outstanding Performance Series. In the end, despite marching season being a train wreck, concert season was a huge success. The future looked bright for the band and its students, and I was eager to continue growing the program in year two.

Jenn became unhappy, though. She felt isolated, being a one-hour drive away from family and friends. In addition, the house we lived in was old, and had countless problems. We reported them to the landlord, but nothing changed. Toward the end of our time in Eden, we developed a terrible mouse infestation. We set traps, and caught seven mice in four hours. Despite keeping everything clean, there were so many holes in the house, that no amount of traps could keep these mice from entering.

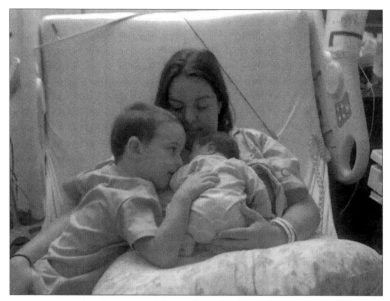

Devin, Jenn, and Kayden the day he was born.

Social media let Jenn forget her loneliness during the day, in particular once she discovered Fitocracy, an online social media platform for fitness. She had already been cooking healthy meals for me again, because I had regained some weight during marching season. Now Jenn finally reached that point where she was sick and tired of being overweight. We bought a treadmill, and she began walking on it every day. She enjoyed logging those walks on Fitocracy, found other likeminded people, and cheered them on each time they posted a workout. It was a great support network for her fitness goals. Still, it wasn't enough.

Adrian, one of my best friends from college, had just landed a job as head band director in a different small town in the area. When the middle school director took another position, he called to offer me her spot. We had always dreamed of working together. There was a Pre-Kindergarten program Devin could attend the next year – which Eden did not have, and our wives were friends. Plus, even though it was only an assistant position, the paycheck was bigger, and we would be living in teacher housing, which was more affordable and better maintained than our current home. I had been looking forward to a second year in Eden, but this felt like the right move for my family.

I don't know if moving was the best decision for my career, but it turned out to be a fantastic decision for my family, especially for Jenn. She was happy to hang out with Adrian's wife, Donna, and felt comfortable opening up to people in town. In no time, she had a strong network of friends.

Our new house was much safer than the one we'd been living in. The boys and I are still there as I write this. It's a three-bedroom house with a living room, small kitchen, dining area, laundry closet, and equipped with two full bathrooms, plus a spacious backyard. It was much more like a home to us. We had begun life together in a tiny office trailer, progressed through the apartment to a sketchy house, and, in the end, a comfortable home. It wasn't ours, but we still felt a sense of accomplishment.

Devin enjoyed Pre-K, and continued to be a happy-go-lucky kid, who was very intelligent, and loved to play. Kayden's second year was much easier than his first, as his fun-loving personality blossomed.

Jenn incorporating Devin into her workouts.

Once we settled in, Jenn found more motivation for her weight loss journey. She read workouts her friends posted on Fitocracy, and researched the exercises, so she could learn to do them correctly. She gradually added these to her routine, and after several months of training, she became a beast. She did squats, wall sits, planks for days, kettlebell workouts, and more.

Then Jenn started a group on Fitocracy called, "Must Plank Heavy Things!" For the cover picture, we had her planking with the coffee table on her back, the boys' little blue recliner on top of that, with Devin sitting in the chair, with Kayden on his lap. After another member trumped that picture, we took one where she was planking me, on her back, both boys lying on me. Her core strength was unreal. And now she was running instead of walking.

Weight loss is transformational. It changed our marriage, as well as Jenn's self-image. She trimmed down substantially, until her face looked like it did in the pictures of her first wedding. There was some loose skin which she hated, but to me she was gorgeous. Everyone else thought the same. She slowly learned to accept the compliments, her confidence at an all-time high. This was the happiest I had ever seen her.

By our second year in Big Lake, Jenn had become a rockstar in the Fitocracy community. Every day, she devoted time to propping – which is a "like" in Facebook terms – people's workouts and leaving comments, encouraging them to keep it up. Everyone in the community loved her positivity and enthusiasm. One tradition was embracing new members and tagging friends to follow them, so they could quickly develop a support network. My wife was constantly getting tagged to follow new people, her reputation for being cheerful and encouraging preceding her. She felt loved and appreciated by this community. This was also about the time she started experimenting with YouTube videos.

We never had cable or satellite TV, so Netflix and Hulu were our substitutes. Eventually, YouTube joined that mix. While I was watching Minecraft videos, Jenn would be looking at makeup tutorials, vloggers and others. She wondered if she could manage creating a channel to generate some income. She published a few videos, but never fully committed. Jenn always had a great sense of humor, which you can see in the early videos with her friends.

Our life was as happy as one could hope for. We were still in love. People commented what a cute couple we were, because they had seen us kissing or flirting, holding hands, cuddling on the couch, and generally behaving like newlyweds. It was normal for us, but we found out that wasn't the case for many couples who had been married for many years. Our boys were both adorable, happy, fun-loving kids, bright and well ahead of the brain development curve. We all had so much fun together.

Devin was in first grade by then. He loved school, excelled at it, and enjoyed hanging out with his friends. Kayden, who had been incredibly difficult during his first year, was sleeping more now, and relished being at home with his mom.

My first year of teaching in this town was a massive struggle. The band students had a very poor experience, and lacked basic music literacy and playing skills. Nothing that worked for me in Eden worked with these students. We had to teach every student from scratch. Thankfully, my second year was substantially better. Half of my varsity band were second-year students we had started the previous year as beginners. They were equal or, in some cases, better players than their 8th-grade counterparts, whom we had "rehabbed" the previous year. It was a good band that ended up earning a couple of Superior ratings in the spring.

Jenn was on fire. Having lost eighty pounds since starting to exercise in Eden, she was more confident in herself than ever. Her fitness level far surpassed mine. She inspired many people to also get in shape. We took pride in having lost over one hundred sixty pounds together. Even dressing up for date night felt cool.

She was an excellent mother. She kept Kayden busy, constantly trying to push his brain to catch on to the next developmental milestone. Her cooking was great. The boys didn't always appreciate it, but I loved it. She also expanded her network of friends in and out of town, so the days of feeling isolated were far behind.

Everything felt perfect. The issues we did have were relatively small. Each one taught us how to communicate more openly and how to resolve problems quickly and efficiently. Sometimes that meant I was wrong, sometimes Jenn had to admit she was wrong, other times we were equally wrong, but every time we questioned ourselves, and put our egos aside to improve our marriage. Even in the first couple of years, when things were rocky, we never yelled at each other or called each other names. That was a ground rule we established from the start. Our love became very deep and strong.

We took great pride and happiness in the feeling of having achieved the dream life we had planned out before Devin was born. We were living on cloud nine, our life as perfect as one can only wish for. Jenn and I were excited to continue building and sharing our lives for several more decades to come.

Jenn and the boys shortly before she was diagnosed.

Chapter 2

Into Hell

"Depression is the inability to construct a future."

– ROLLO MAY

O N THE NIGHT of Wednesday, March 12, 2014, Jenn and I were getting ready for bed. She was spending longer than usual in the bathroom. When she came out, everything seemed normal. I fell asleep, not knowing that what she had been examining in the bathroom had irreversibly changed our lives forever.

The next morning, as we were lying in bed, Jenn looked at me with a grim face and said, "There's something I need to show you. But promise me you won't freak out."

"I'll try. What's going on?" I responded.

"I want you to feel my breast." I freaked out. Every woman in Jenn's family on her mother's side had fought breast cancer. But she was only thirty-one years old. We figured it might happen in her forties or fifties, but this early seemed preposterous. She reached over, took my hand, then carefully placed it on her right breast. I clearly felt a golf ball sized lump, and the area was discolored like a light bruise. I was horrified.

"Is that breast cancer?" I asked, assuming the worst.

33

"I don't know for sure. It could be something else, but my gut tells me it is." She was keeping her calm much better than I was. To be fair, she had had a little time to process it.

"I thought you checked yourself monthly. How did you just now catch this?" I regretted the words as soon as I said them. To this day I wish I could take them back. It was not her fault, and there was nothing she could have done. But a part of me could not believe how massive this growth was, and how she could have missed it.

"I do check myself monthly. I'm pretty sure I did..." Now I felt worse.

"Okay, we need to get you to a doctor as soon as possible," I said. Part of my crisis management mode is to start finding solutions quickly.

"I'll call the clinic in town and schedule an appointment today." She meant a hospital in San Angelo. We did not trust one particular doctor in our small town, so to make sure to never encounter him again, we always drove the extra hour to San Angelo for any medical needs.

I felt a bit better. We had a plan of action. Jenn was not shying away from having it examined. I calmed down enough to apologize for freaking out, and for being a jerk. Unfortunately, I had to get ready for work, but the conversation stayed on my mind all day.

Jenn had been able to get an appointment the same day. When I got home, we sat down in the bedroom, away from the kids, and she told me what had happened. Her doctor did not say it was cancer, but looked very concerned when she touched the lump, and insisted on rushing Jenn through the diagnostic process. She set up an appointment for the following Wednesday at the Women's Imaging Center in San Angelo.

Every day of waiting felt like sitting on top of a ticking time bomb. We fervently hoped Jenn did not have cancer, but what if she did? If she did, it was already eating away at her body and she needed to start treatment yesterday. The wait was excruciating. What about our future? Could it please *not* be cancer?

The day we went to the Imaging Center was incredibly emotional. It started at eight in the morning. I had taken off from work, and her mom, Cindy, came with us. We both wanted to be there for Jenn.

The team at the Imaging Center was amiable and worked with great efficiency. Right after Jenn finished filling out paperwork, she was taken back for mammograms. She later told us they had to take an additional picture of her right breast, and then two more, magnified. The technician tried to reassure her by saying she had seen cysts this large and that she would be fine, but then asked if Jenn had any friends in town and stressed the importance of having friends during times like these. *Times like these?* We felt affirmed in our suspicions and hope began to fade.

Immediately after the mammograms came sonograms. Here the diagnostician told Jenn that, yes, it was cancer. She explained the difference between a cyst and cancer, and that the images matched a cancer diagnosis. Additionally, some lymph nodes under Jenn's right arm were cause for concern, because once the disease spreads to the lymphatic system, it becomes dangerous. The physician also explained they were going to take a biopsy, which would identify the type of cancer and what the treatment plan should be. When Jenn conveyed this information to us, it was a devastating blow. My only thought was, "What now?"

They then took an MRI of her breasts, drew blood and performed the biopsy. All of this happened before lunch.

The staff even set up a consultation with a surgeon in San Antonio. We felt extremely fortunate to have gone to that imaging center on that particular day. They fast-tracked Jenn through the process, which was crucial, because every day without treatment gave the cancer time to grow. And it was expanding at an aggressive rate.

As if having to deal with the nightmare diagnosis wasn't enough, this horror scenario also had a financial aspect. Not all the tests were covered by our health insurance, due to Jenn's age. In America, health insurance companies believe you can be too young to have breast cancer, and will deny payment until you hit the statistically appropriate age. If you dare get sick too early, you have to pay out of your own pocket.

In the middle of this already surreal day, Jenn received a call from Laura Bush, the daughter of former President George W. Bush. She was letting us know that the Laura Bush Foundation would pay for the biopsy, which was not only a huge relief, but also kind of cool. The kind staff at the imaging center had submitted forms to the charity on our behalf.

We spent the rest of the day crying, recounting the events, talking about the treatment plan over and over again, trying to reassure ourselves everything was going to be okay. I wanted to be strong for Jenn, so I tried to keep my composure. Her mom was very emotional, but agreed to watch Kayden for a few days to give us time to process the situation.

At some point Jenn declared in a bitter voice, "This cancer is going to kill me." She was already pissed off about it. I refused to go there. Despite her uncanny ability to predict the future, by the end of the day, she was determined to fight and do everything necessary to beat it. Still, she was terrified, not just of dying, but the treatment. Having been the caretaker – along with her step-dad – when her mom fought cancer, and knowing how sick one gets in the process, made her not want to go through that, nor have the boys witness it. She had a much better understanding of the direction our lives would be taking than I did. I wanted to be strong, not let it bother me, and do anything to help her fight this disease so we could grow old together.

"Whatever it takes." That was our plan. And that is what we did.

Waiting for test results is incredibly stressful. There is this impending sense of doom, leaving you in limbo to make futile plans until the verdict is in. This feeling of dire uncertainty is almost impossible to tolerate, but there is no choice. You have no control and that makes it unbearable.

We did receive an overwhelming amount of phone calls and messages of love and support, which was amazing. I heard from friends I hadn't been in touch with for months, even years, and Jenn had so many more reaching out to her.

In addition, our friend Donna had started an online fundraiser to help cover the cost of a critical test we had to pay for out of pocket. We needed to raise three thousand dollars to find out whether her cancer was due to a genetic defect. Friends and family smashed through that goal within a week or two.

We had never felt so much love, support and compassion, but there was no denying the catastrophic, life-altering news. It was an emotional roller coaster, any reprieve merely temporary. No matter how high people raised our spirits, we would inescapably drop back down into the black pit that is cancer.

It was critical to find out the specific type of Jenn's cancer. There are several, but they fall into two major groups – one with an eighty percent chance of successful treatment, the other close to zero percent. We knew – thought we knew, anyway, in reality we had no clue – that if it would turn out to be a "traditional" breast cancer, Jenn could beat it and eventually be okay. Able to find the positive in any situation, she joked about the new and better boobs she would be getting.

If it was inflammatory or triple negative breast cancer, we knew we were screwed, and, at the very least, in for an even more difficult road. Jenn's instinct told her it was triple negative, based on the fast growth rate and the appearance of her breast.

Once again, Jenn's prediction became fact. We received the call a few days after our trip to the imaging center. These were only preliminary results, but the bottom-line: it was early, very aggressive, triple negative breast cancer. More details were to follow.

Every single time we got test results, we cried. Occasionally tears of relief, but more often tears of sorrow, followed by a deeper sense of impending doom.

Researching survival rates for patients with stage 2 triple negative breast cancer was a big mistake. I only found one study, and it wasn't hopeful. It said fifty percent of patients died within the first year after diagnosis, about twenty-five percent would survive the second year, ten percent the third. The five year survival rate in this study was zero percent. Statistics change, but it was the best information available to me at the time. I was a mess the next day at work. And many days after that.

Jenn and I agreed it would be ok to cry together, though we rarely did. When one of us fell apart, the other would stay strong to provide comfort. Not that it was easy. Seeing her so vulnerable and hopeless broke my heart.

I realized what a fairy tale our life had been, the kind people dream of. An incredible marriage supposed to last forever, happy children who knew they were loved, and returned that love in abundance. My career was going well. We had worked hard for this life, wanted to keep it, build on it, and this diagnosis threatened to destroy it all. Sure, we still had family and friends who loved us, but our entire world was turned upside down. Cancer had already robbed us of any sense of security, and over time it would take away so much more. I knew it was going to be difficult, but I had no idea of the hell that was to come.

Next we had to wait to see the specialist in San Antonio. He was supposedly one of the best in the entire state, which became irrelevant when the hospital called to inform us that he was not part of our insurance network. Our health plan charged lesser premiums, but had fewer physicians to choose from, and this specialist was not one of them. We were on our own.

After hours of frustrating conversations with the insurance company, we settled on the Scott & White Hospital in Temple, Texas. Other cancer patients online reassured us that it was one of the top three facilities in the state and that their doctors were world class. We scheduled a consultation as soon as possible, but it still meant more time would pass before Jenn could begin treatment. Tick, tick, tick.

The consultation happened to be on the day my middle school band had to give their most important performance of the year at the regional concert and sight-reading contest. Passion for my job came second only to passion for my family, so it was difficult for me not to be there. Adrian took the band on my behalf and led them through the day. One of the students and his mom bought small pink ribbons, which all the kids wore on their uniforms, in solidarity for Jenn, who was feeling guilty. She knew I had worked on this contest all year. I assured her I was right where I belonged, but a big part of me really wanted to be there. This would be the first of many times the cancer disrupted my work routine.

The Scott & White Hospital felt different the moment you walked in. Other hospitals in West Texas appeared old in comparison. This place belonged in a medical drama. We met

Jenn's surgeon and her oncologist, both of whom were a bit odd, but clearly super intelligent. They told us her case had been presented to a panel consisting of all cancer related specialists at the hospital, and together they had formulated a treatment plan. Chemotherapy, followed by surgery, then radiation to clean up whatever was left.

There was both good and bad news about her cancer. On the upside, triple negative breast cancer usually responded extremely well to chemotherapy. But, if Jenn made it to remission, there was no treatment available to prevent its return. Even worse, in case it did come back, it was terminal. However, assuming she stayed in remission for five years, it almost certainly would not return. Jenn's cancer was also highly aggressive, with a ninety-eight percent growth rate. The doctors impressed upon us it would not be easy, but that if we did everything they asked, she had a chance to survive.

More waiting until her first chemotherapy treatment. Part of me was still torn about missing work to take Jenn to appointments. I *hated* missing classes. The middle school band program is a two-person job. With one of us absent, the students make less progress, so every day it happens is time in their development we can't recover. I knew, even without Adrian's constant reassurance, I was doing the right thing by being at Jenn's side. She needed me, and I refused to let her walk this path alone. I hated how everything was changing. Our entire lives revolved around fighting this cancer.

It was disruptive for the boys, too. Once we felt ready, we told them about the cancer, omitting details of how dangerous it was. You can't hide it, so we made sure they knew mommy was going to be sick for a long time, what to expect regarding us being away for appointments a lot, and how it all would affect them. We wanted the boys to miss as little school as possible, so we arranged for a friend to pick them up after class and babysit until our return. Whenever we had to go to Temple, it meant an overnight trip. The kids missed us and felt sad having to be with a sitter so often.

Starting chemotherapy was scary. The medication, often a combination of drugs, circulates through the patient's entire body, attacking cancer cells, which grow and divide quickly. Unfortunately, it also kills fast-growing healthy cells. This is why people lose their hair, experience nausea, vomiting, diarrhea, neuropathy, and numerous other side effects.

We were both a nervous wreck on the drive into town for Jenn's first treatment. Fortunately, she was permitted to do them in San Angelo, four hours closer than Temple. When we weren't vaping our electronic cigarettes, we were holding hands. The thought of Jenn having poison pumped into her body sickened me, and we felt extremely anxious, wondering which of the numerous potential side effects she would have to grapple with.

At the cancer treatment center, we met her local oncologist, a sweet and caring man. He would end up being her primary cancer physician, due to the close rapport they developed over time. Until then, he merely carried out the orders from Jenn's team in Temple.

I had heard of treatment facilities with private infusion rooms. This was not one of them. After our consultation with the oncologist, we walked into the treatment room. Picture a large, shoebox-shaped area with at least two dozen infusion chairs, most of them occupied by older patients. The majority of those patients sat alone. The lucky ones had a spouse or someone else at their side. All of them looked miserable. My anxiety increased. I just couldn't believe Jenn was about to endure the same treatment they were.

As the procedure went on, I hated every step. I hated seeing Jenn sit in the chair, getting poked in the arm to insert the IV, I hated when they brought each bag, especially the first bag of chemotherapy, and hooked it up to her body. I watched as each bag dripped into the tube attached to her arm, the liquid slowly making its way into her bloodstream. It was horrible. She was being poisoned. But that poison was the best weapon we had against her cancer.

Jenn tried to make light of the situation by joking around with the staff. She appeared brave, but I wasn't buying any of it. She had to be more terrified than her mother, who was also there, and myself. I just wanted it to stop. I tried my best not to let it get to me, but it did. By the end of the infusion, I felt mentally and physically sick. Jenn got through it like a champ.

Afterward, Jenn wanted to eat, so we went to a deli. It took some time, but we eventually unwound. Jenn dozed off on the car ride home, and would be mostly asleep and in pain for the next two or three days. Our first taste of chemo side effects. The boys and I hated seeing her so weak and in agony. It was depressing, especially considering we had another fifteen rounds to go. With each successive treatment, the side effects were expected to accumulate, become more intense, and last longer. I began to understand how awful this road was going to be.

That statistic for triple negative breast cancer – zero percent survival rate after five years – haunted me. The thought of Jenn dying freaked me out and became all-consuming. I began to feel as though my entire universe was collapsing in on me. Knowing she was likely to die made everything spin out of control, the same way I imagine the planets would if the sun were to suddenly disappear.

I envisioned a future in which I was lifeless. I pictured myself after my wife's death as a person with no energy or motivation. Would I be able to hang on to the career I had worked so hard to achieve? What kind of father would I be on my own? Would I be so broken by the loss of my great love that I could hardly be a father at all, much less the father I needed to be? What if my kids felt neglected on top of having lost their mom, and grew up to be terrible people, maybe drug addicts or who knows what? My children are incredible, mind you. I have much more faith in them, but lacked the confidence in myself.

During the first year and a half of Jenn's cancer battle, as time went on, I slowly became less motivated and capable. I was extremely stressed and found helping around the house difficult. At a time when I should have buckled down to be stronger than ever, when my family really needed me, I chose instead to sit on my butt. I had found an escape, the computer game Minecraft.

I was angry and bitter about losing the great life we had worked so long and hard to achieve. This manifested in different ways. Primarily I became less patient. I managed to retain my patience with Jenn, but it was a lot more difficult with my children, as well as my students. Fortunately, having gone through therapy at age twelve, I had generally been a calm person. I was never outright mean to my students, but tolerated a lot less crap. For example, they found it was much easier to get sent to the principal's office now. Depending on the offense and the number of times they had been there before, it could mean just a talking to, or getting swats. And I honestly didn't care. They shouldn't have been breaking the band hall rules to begin with, so as far as I was concerned, those repercussions were on them. But before and after Jenn's cancer, I worked harder to talk to the students and tried coaching them into changing their behaviors in class.

Though I hate to admit it, I was a lot less patient with my own kids. It made me feel guilty, because this was the time they needed their dad the most. Those little guys love me with every fiber of their being. I am a hero in their eyes. So, whenever I was impatient or mean, it had a devastating impact.

Mainly it just meant being short if they were misbehaving or not giving me the space I badly needed. The constant stress I was under made it difficult to remain calm, especially when the boys were endlessly asking for things or wanting attention. I swear I was doing the very best I could.

There is a song by Coheed and Cambria called *Eraser*, in which the lead singer, Claudio Sanchez, describes wishing he could turn back time to when he hadn't been so mean. He sings about being a happy kid, and never wanting to turn out like this, and I related to that so much. I didn't like being a mean teacher and certainly not a mean parent, but just couldn't stop myself. One of the many frustrating changes that can happen to you when you're depressed or going through a grieving process.

Jenn experienced the opposite. She had typically been the one prone to overreacting and having a short fuse – although she had already improved a lot since we left Eden. Cancer changed Jenn's perspective. She realized how trivial our old problems had been, how our children's small transgressions deserved more love and patience. Our roles had reversed.

My work began to suffer. Not only was I missing at least one day every two weeks, but my energy plummeted. I felt guilty all the time, especially being a teacher. Classical music and music education used to be such a huge passion for me, that I had struggled to prioritize my family. Back then, after coming home from work, I immediately reflected on my classes and set goals for the next day, eager to improve my teaching skills. Sometimes I even wrote about my experiences in a blog.

Once I began considering life without Jenn, none of it mattered anymore. I did not want to be a bad teacher. It wasn't the students' fault I was going through depression, and they deserved better. So I did what I could, trying hard to make my band students as successful as possible. But I had less to give, and for more than two years, they did not get my best. I wondered if my passion would return, or if it was gone forever.

Cancer patients have an expression. When they start forgetting things, they blame it on the side effects of chemotherapy. "Sorry, I have chemo brain." We as caregivers, and anybody who's loved one is going through this, should be allowed a similar excuse when our memory is not what it should be. I call it "trauma brain."

46

I've always had a sharp memory. In high school, I participated in the Air Force Junior ROTC Corps, which is a program designed to foster analytical skills, teamwork and physical fitness. I memorized everything, from the name of every cadet and their duties, to all of the awards you could earn along with their requirements, and used that to excel as an officer.

In college, I knew every operational detail of my fraternity, which was Kappa Kappa Psi, National Honorary Band Fraternity. I had memorized the Chapter, District, and National Constitutions. When I was elected Chapter President, I leveraged my extensive knowledge, to ensure our chapter met as many award requirements as possible. We didn't win that year, but we reached the finals and made a huge impression at our District Convention. The committee even created a new award for the following year, based on our efforts, called, "Most Improved Chapter Award."

I was able to remember the exact words used in a conversation, dates for upcoming events, you name it. Until Jenn got cancer. Once she was diagnosed, when I saw the zero percent chance of survival, my world spun out of control, and that ability was gone. Maybe, because nothing else mattered to me, it wasn't worth memorizing. Or perhaps my brain was already so overloaded, trying to process our situation, that it had no capacities left.

I would get so angry with myself for not being able to remember stuff. Having a good memory was something I had been proud of, and losing that was infuriating.

Depression is like living in a bubble surrounded by thick fog. You don't notice any of the good things going on around you, because the fog obscures them. All you see, and feel, is pain. Sometimes that pain is empathy for your loved ones, who are also dealing with this loss, or if your spouse is still alive, the empathy with them. After a while, it becomes your normal state of being. It may seem like it's all you'll ever feel again.

Over time, it got more difficult to cry around Jenn. It happened once in a while, but it felt safer for me to cry in the car. I had to run to the store almost daily for supplies, one of the few times I was alone, and whenever that opportunity occurred, I could barely control myself. Like when you have to pee, but can't right now, so you hold it in. Then, the moment you get to a restroom, it's as if your brain signals your bladder, and you can barely reach the toilet in time. This may be a strange analogy, but me crying in the car felt like that. On my way to the car, the tears came, often before I had even opened the door.

The car was my safe place. It was also where I listened to music, which can make it easier to let your feelings come out. I didn't know much about grieving, but it helped me get through some really bad days.

Typically when I had listened to the radio, to what classical musicians refer to as popular music, I hadn't been able to relate to the lyrics. I didn't seem to have the problems most singers vocalized. I liked music that sounded cool to me, perhaps with a catchy rhythm or an interesting chord progression, but be it rock or rap, I cared about the instrumentals and the melody, not the lyrics. Jenn was the complete opposite. Now though, I could suddenly relate to popular music. The album I gravitated toward was *The Color Before the Sun* by Coheed and Cambria, which had just been released, along with a couple of their older tracks. Some of the songs on that album talked about losing a loved one. I had listened to their music for years, but this was the first time I could truly relate. It was cathartic.

When Jenn was diagnosed, I had been playing the video game Minecraft for over a year. I had just started making videos for it, inspired by other YouTubers, who managed to teach viewers lessons about the game, and be entertaining at the same time. Later on I co-founded a server exclusively for YouTubers, called The Diamond Society. I hoped my videos would inspire people to play the game, just like I had been.

Minecraft became my escape during this period in the cancer journey. Any free moment I had, I hopped onto a server. It is an exceptionally immersive game, because you spawn into a randomly generated world, but can change everything, creating a unique place, by custom landscaping and building structures of any size and style. The only limit is your imagination. Through Minecraft I was able to visit another world, one where cancer did not exist.

Between playing the game and video editing, it provided a much-needed escape for me, for as many as forty hours a week.

Everywhere I went, my laptop went with me. That way, when we made overnight trips to Temple for consultation, I was able to play in the hotel room. Once chemotherapy started, I was on Minecraft while Jenn was either knocked out from the Benadryl or talking to friends or her mom, who came to visit her almost every treatment.

I know it sounds excessive. The guilt about playing so much, when I could have been doing housework, or spending more time with the boys instead, nagged at me. But I needed that outlet. Jenn's condition was too much to process all at once. I had to handle it in small chunks if I wanted to prevent a complete mental collapse.

Minecraft is excellent escapism, yet it's also a great place to make friends. Later, when Jenn was soliciting donations for her bucket list, they even pooled their money for a group contribution. Words cannot express how helpful it was to be able to play the game with other people, friendly adults who were willing to let me vent, or just talk about the game to get my mind off the tragic reality.

Even though I had Minecraft and music, it wasn't enough. Jenn had not received a terminal diagnosis yet, still I could not get that study showing a zero percent survival rate after five years out of my head. I tried to stay optimistic, to give Jenn strength and confidence, but in the back of my mind I knew the cancer would likely kill her. Less than a month into treatment, I was losing my mind trying to comprehend the fact that my wife was probably going to die. When I wasn't playing Minecraft, I was extremely stressed. The moment I turned it off, the weight of it all came crushing down on me. I wasn't allowing myself enough time or space to deal with it. Ten to fifteen minutes in the car wasn't enough.

I had to find a way to get my stress level under control. So, I did what I always do in a crisis – research. Meditation caught my eye.

I had always been interested, but never given it a real chance. At this point, I was ready to try anything, so why not meditation? I read many articles giving advice on how to sit, how to breathe and what to think about, if you plan to think about anything at all.

The primary goal of meditation is to learn to accept reality as it is, rather than what you want it to be, or perceive it to be. You take things the way they are, without labeling them as good or bad. It just is what it is. You become a passive observer of the present. This lets your mind move away from the past, a happy life in my case, and away from the future, which was full of darkness, to focus on what is happening right now.

Becoming more aware of my body and surroundings, learning to live in the moment, helped improve my coping skills. I realized Jenn wasn't dead yet. Jenn was here, our family was still together. I knew it was going to get worse, but now, whenever these thoughts popped into my head, I was able to redirect them back to living in the present. It allowed me to appreciate whatever was good at that moment. I found a sense of calm, and while I still experienced breakdowns, I had a new tool to deal with them. Instead of falling apart completely, I recognized it as suffering, watching it pass through me, until I felt "normal" again.

In one type of meditation you sit quietly, and just observe what happens without judgment. In Vipassana – the most difficult and intense for me – you focus on physical sensations. It can be discomfort, an itching or tingling. When you experience that, you do not move or do anything to fix it. You merely make a mental note of it. How intense is it? What area is it happening in? How long does it last? You do not judge it as good or bad. It just is.

Similarly, you can observe emotions, whether they're pleasant or not. What emotion are you feeling? How intense is it? Is the intensity changing? What physical sensations accompany this feeling? Again, don't try to change or judge it. You simply let it be. You become like someone standing in a river, allowing the emotions to flow through and pass you by.

Making no effort to alter the physical or emotional sensations is an essential aspect of the mental training. Every time you experience something, it changes, and eventually goes away. Through your own repeated experiences, you come to understand that everything is continually evolving, and nothing lasts forever. An incredible life lesson. I used this method to help me accept that Jenn could, and probably would, die, and that my life would never be the same. Everything changes – constantly.

It also allowed me to feel the emotional pain, rather than hide from it. Crying became an old friend. Whenever I felt overwhelmed, I let those emotions come out through tears, and did not see them as negative. It just is what it is, and you let it run its course. This way, the feelings can pass through you instead of building up inside.

One very critical piece of advice I would give to anyone who is grieving – you have to learn to be okay with crying, and the emotions and physical sensations that go along with it. Do not associate it with anything negative. Allow it to be what it is, to become like an old friend. Because once it's over, you will feel a huge sense of relief.

Turning crying and other manifestations of grief into positive acts was extremely useful in helping me cope as well as I did. I don't cry very often these days, but when the sadness does creep up on me, I don't mind it. Meditation showed me that grief is healing, not painful.

My introspective journey eventually led me to Buddhism. I had stopped believing in God several years prior to Jenn's diagnosis. My parents raised me Christian, and I struggled with my faith for a long time before giving it up. Jenn held onto her Christian beliefs for several months into the cancer battle. It was never an issue in our marriage. Buddhism seemed like a revelation to me. I was studying and practicing for a while, and found it beneficial.

Then I hit a roadblock. After months of meditation, I had to conclude that Buddhism would not work for me. The goal of Buddhism is to free yourself from the cycle of misery, and a major part is learning to release yourself from attachment. While I could detach from many things, I refused to let go of the attachment to my family. If I couldn't complete the path of Buddhism, it made no sense to continue following it. Perhaps a mentor could have helped me through that, since there are happily married Buddhists. I was unable to find the answers, so my journey ended here.

I did continue to meditate, if not as frequently. Be advised that certain schools claim their form of meditation is the best for whatever reason. But just like one religion does not work for the billions of individuals in the world, no one type of meditation is going to be right for everybody. In the end, I was able to pick from a variety of coping techniques I had learned, and use the one most beneficial to each situation.

After a few months of chemotherapy, it was time for surgery. Jenn required a double mastectomy, which is the removal of both breasts. Traditionally, the entire breasts are taken off, leaving women flat-chested, with massive scars. Jenn's surgeon at Scott & White in Temple, who appeared like the kind of rockstar surgeon you would see on a TV medical drama, suggested a skin-sparing double mastectomy instead. Not every physician has the training to pull this off. In this procedure, they create a small round opening by removing the nipples, then scoop out all the breast tissue from inside, leaving the skin in place. The benefits are minimal scarring, faster recovery, and that later breast reconstruction is easier and more aesthetically pleasing. The downside is that Jenn would be left with bunched up, loose skin on her chest, but this was supposed to only be temporary.

Cancer has few positive consequences, but Jenn had been looking forward to replacing her natural breasts with fake, perkier ones. The skin-sparing surgery would allow her new breasts to look and feel more natural. While Jenn's surgeon was fully confident in her abilities – as were we – her local oncologist in San Angelo took a staunch stance against it, recommending a radical mastectomy. His fear was that with the skin left in place, if any of the skin cells had been invaded, it would cause remission, moving Jenn to Stage IV. He warned us of having had several patients who had elected to have this surgery, only to have the cancer return later. Jenn's surgeon rebutted that there was no evidence of skin-sparing double mastectomy being tied to higher rates of recurrence than the traditional surgery, so we decided to trust her judgment and go that route.

I have questioned the decision since then. Did we make the wrong call, or would Jenn have had a recurrence anyway? Those thoughts are ultimately meaningless to dwell on, since you can't go back in time to find out.

Close family and friends assembled in Jenn's hospital room. We were all on edge about the operation, and Jenn tried to lighten the mood by offering to "motorboat" me one last time. When the surgical team came to retrieve her, it was difficult for me to remain composed. What if this was the last time I saw her? Surgeries are never without risk, but Jenn had nearly died giving birth to Kayden due to an error by the anesthesiologist. We kept our fingers crossed and anxiously sat in the waiting room.

Thankfully, at this hospital, they updated the family at least once an hour. We did our best to make small talk, or otherwise keep our minds preoccupied. To everyone's relief, the operation was a success. Jenn's surgeon visited afterward to inform us that she had retrieved one hundred percent of the breast tissue, and found no other evidence of cancer. They had also removed a few of the lymph nodes in her right arm pit.

While Jenn was in the recovery room, we received training on caring for the drainage tubes running out of her chest. For a couple of weeks it was my job to empty the pouches as needed, keeping a journal of how much fluid had collected, and to rinse and clean the tubes before reinserting them. We spent another night in a nearby hotel, so Jenn wouldn't have to endure the road until she'd had the chance to heal at least a little bit. Gradually, over the next few months, she recovered her normal range of motion through daily exercises.

This felt like a major victory to us. Jenn was one major step closer to being cancer free.

Once Jenn had recovered from the operation, radiation was scheduled. Although chemotherapy had greatly reduced the size of the tumor, and surgery had successfully removed all detectable cancer cells, it was possible that additional malignant cells lay dormant, or were traveling around her body, looking for a new area to latch onto. Radiation was the clean up crew of the treatment plan.

It was a *lot* of appointments. Daily radiation to her torso, Monday through Friday, for four weeks. Because we lived an hour away from the treatment center, Jenn was faced with the decision of driving back and forth each day, or staying with her mom during the week. She chose the latter, because, like chemotherapy, radiation side effects accumulate. Among other issues, it meant that Jenn would be progressively more exhausted following each session, so it seemed wise for her to have a short distance to travel. Short enough so other people could take her if necessary. Financially it made sense as well.

The downside was that I would be home alone with the boys except on the weekends, when Jenn came home to visit. Devin, Kayden and I missed her immensely, and she us, but we spoke daily on the phone, or by video chat whenever possible. Besides, we all knew we were apart for an important reason – to ensure Jenn had the best chance of being cancer free for the rest of her life. We held onto that hope. Once radiation was over, so was cancer treatment, and with it the end of many months of physical hell for Jenn, and emotional hell for the family.

I had stemmed the tide that had been crushing my mental health long enough to get us through chemotherapy, surgery, and radiation. Remission, the doctors said. We could breathe again. I was even starting to feel stressed about work. But a few months later, Jenn began experiencing new pains, and sure enough, it was the cancer. It had spread. She was now considered Stage IV, and terminal. It showed up on her diaphragm and in her brain. She was screwed. Our life together was going to end, and all we could do was delay the inevitable.

My coping mechanisms of music, gaming and meditation were not enough. Jenn started new rounds of chemotherapy. This time she deteriorated faster than before. Her physical and mental condition hit an all-time low. The boys and I suffered with her. The worse she got, the worse we felt. I did everything I could to keep it together, but none of my previous coping strategies were working. Jenn was going to die. It wasn't just a thought in the back of my head anymore, it was reality.

I was losing my mind, more deeply this time, pushing me closer to the brink of a mental collapse. Jenn's symptoms continually got worse, and none of the scans were ever good news anymore. We found ourselves in a downward spiral of mental deterioration, culminating the night I completely broke, when she was in so much pain, she told me to let her die if possible. I had finally called a therapist, begging for help. That night marked the end of me being trapped in hell and the beginning of my long journey through it.

Chapter 3

The Path Through

"The only way out is through."

– ROBERT FROST

THERAPY WAS THE single most important factor in getting through my depression and grief. The Alpha Behavioral Center in Odessa, Texas, called me back the very next day after I had left that desperate voicemail on their machine. They had openings, and I took the first available one, even though it meant I had to take time off work. But so what? I knew I couldn't handle this by myself any longer. I needed professional help.

I have been incredibly lucky with the therapists I've had. The one I saw when I was twelve changed my life. I had been very angry at the time. I was hiding the depth of my anger from my dad and step-mom, but at school, around my friends, I let it all out. My therapist helped me identify the source of my anxiety and stress, and taught me a few coping skills. Through her, I learned how to forgive, and what a powerful life lesson that was. The change wasn't immediate, but after about six months of weekly, hour-long appointments, one day I suddenly realized how different I felt. I had more patience, more appreciation for my parents, and things didn't bother me as easily.

So I knew from my previous experience, there were at least two conditions for making therapy work. First, you have to go on a regular basis, consistently. We lived out in the middle of the oil patch, in a small town without mental health services. The closest city providing them was a ninety minute drive away. That meant I always had to take a day off, when I was already missing a lot of work to go with Jenn to her treatment and consultation appointments. Toward the end, I had to start relying more on other people willing to accompany her. Many of my coworkers had even donated some of their personal days, so my pay would not get docked.

I scheduled therapy sessions to be once every other week. Less than that felt insufficient. I would have gone every week, and probably seen faster results, but it just wasn't possible. Again though, the important part was to commit to a schedule and to not let anything get in the way.

Second, I knew I wasn't going to feel better overnight. It takes several sessions to build the kind of trust with your therapist that allows you to explore those deeper issues in just one hour. Even if it seemed entirely futile at times, I had to keep going, believing it would eventually work.

I wanted Jenn to come to therapy with me, but she wasn't interested. In part, because she'd had bad luck with therapists in her past, but she also said, "I'm dying anyway. What difference does it make?" I argued that if it helped her come to terms with what she was going through, then she might be able to enjoy life more fully while she still could, rather than feeling depressed all the time. But Jenn didn't budge, and I had to be okay with that.

There I was, at my new therapist's office, sitting on a comfortable couch surrounded by posters with affirmations and life lessons. What was I going to say? Or ask?

Misty walked in with a warm smile. We introduced ourselves, and she said she was excited to meet me after all the great things my dad had told her about me. I didn't know how to start, so I explained our cancer story up to that point. But before I left, I needed help with a particular problem.

I carried a lot of guilt about my decreasing capabilities around the house and at work. I was being lazy, even though I knew I needed to be strong for my wife and children. When I shared this with my therapist, her answer surprised me.

"Don't beat yourself up," Misty said, "It may not seem like it, Chris, but you're doing an amazing job of coping in an incredibly difficult situation. A lot of people would have shut down or checked out by now, but you still have your job, are there for your wife and present for your kids. You're doing – awesome."

While I did not agree with that assessment, it did help me feel better to hear a professional say it. She went on to explain that I was only human, not Superman, and that the depression was the reason I couldn't do as much as I used to. She said it was normal, natural, and most importantly, "...not a reflection of your character."

Not a reflection of your character. Those words changed everything. I had beaten myself up for months about not getting more accomplished, without even considering the status of my mental health. Misty reassured me that as long as I was able to hang on to my job, provide for my family, and be available to them, the rest didn't matter.

This allowed me to relax a bit, forgive myself and start figuring out how to be okay with my current situation. I had to accept that, while I was depressed, I wouldn't be as capable as I used to be. I learned to be gentle with myself, to give myself a pass. It was the opening my psyche needed to start repairing some of the damage this trauma had caused.

At the end of our first session, I told her I had issues before Jenn's cancer, which I was also willing to address, and she asked me to type up a summary of my life story. I was ready to get to work.

To get the most out of therapy, I determined to be as honest as possible about my life and feelings right from the start, full disclosure. After all, if I forced Misty to pry the information out of me, I was wasting my time and money, neither of which I had to spare.

Acquiring self-reflection skills was especially useful in my recovery. When you're not feeling well, it helps to self-analyze your mental state and find the root of your fears. Ultimately, all negative emotions stem from fear. This realization came as part of a huge breakthrough several months into therapy. Once you've identified the fear, you can address it, which reduces anxiety and improves your mood.

Misty is a wonderful therapist, highly respected by her peers, and I consider myself lucky to have been one of her patients. She had previously worked with people who had lost loved ones, but never with someone like me, stuck in the limbo of knowing they were going to lose their spouse in the near future.

Misty helped me in a variety of ways. She looked at the coping mechanisms I had been getting by with, and found them to be normal and acceptable. For example, my excessive Minecraft playing. She explained that it wasn't irresponsible, but common and even necessary to have ways to escape reality, so I could process what was happening in smaller, safer chunks. If gaming helped, I should continue. I was officially under "doctor's orders" to play Minecraft. Her validation of what I had done to maintain my sanity thus far, that I wasn't a bad person because of it, meant a lot to me.

She also taught me new coping strategies, and showed me how to implement them by setting goals. One such goal was to get back in touch with old friends, so I could have people I trusted to vent to, and to make it a point to call them regularly. I started phoning friends on the drive home, right after I left her office that day.

The goals changed from week to week. If I had read about this technique in a book or on the internet, and tried to execute it on my own, I doubt I would've been successful. Many times I didn't even start working on a goal until days before my next therapy session. The bi-weekly appointments provided a strong incentive for me to do something that would improve my mental health.

Misty also helped me take care of other tasks I had been neglecting. We talked about antidepressants, and I admitted how terrible I was at scheduling doctor visits for myself. So she offered to do it for me. Who knew that was even possible? All I had to do was sign a form permitting her to act on my behalf. Not long after, I went to my first primary care doctor's appointment as an adult. The office also researched the best child grief specialist for the boys. I cannot emphasize enough the positive impact a good therapist can have, especially if you are consistent and apply yourself for an extended period of time.

There exists a preconceived notion that therapy is only for the weak, or the mentally ill. Two comments on that. First, I believe everyone should have a good therapist, to have a professional to vent to, get advice from, and assist in their personal growth. Can you imagine how much better this world would be, if we all had a Misty?

Second, if you're struggling to keep it together, you must put your ego aside and seek help, especially if there is someone depending on you. I had reached a point where I didn't care what I had to do, or what pills I had to take. It was paramount, far more important than my stupid ego, to be able to hold onto my job and support my wife and children. Pride can be a great hindrance, but you need to overcome it. It takes real strength to admit weakness. The biggest regret about my journey through grief is not accepting professional help sooner.

I had serious reservations about antidepressants. I never even liked taking aspirin or ibuprofen, I always thought it was best to let the body handle as much as it could naturally, disregarding any potential discomfort. So the idea of a drug that might alter my personality took some getting used to.

One evening, Jenn, the boys and I went to a family dinner out of town. My grandparents were also there. Grandma twice experienced the loss of a spouse. Her first husband committed suicide after returning from World War II with what was surely undiagnosed post-traumatic stress disorder. He left her a widow with *five* daughters to raise. She somehow found the strength to persevere, and eventually got married to the man I called Grandpa for almost forty years, until he too passed away. Devastated all over again, she still refused to succumb to grief and happily keeps on going to this day. My grandma truly is a woman of amazing inner strength and wisdom.

Not long before this dinner, we had been given the news that Jenn's cancer was back, had spread, and would be fatal. It took some courage on my part, but I managed to ask Grandma, "How did you do it? How did you move on and find happiness again?"

Her answer was blunt, and she started out by telling me terrible details I had been unaware of. "Did you know that he shot himself in the front yard of the house?"

"No, I hadn't heard that part."

"Yes, and you would think that when they come to take the body, they would help clean up the mess. But nobody did. So once everyone was gone, I had to go through the yard and pick up the pieces of him that were left. No one helped me." I was speechless. "The first thing I would say is that you need to take antidepressants as soon as possible. Start them now. Don't wait until it gets so bad you can't come back. I was lucky to have a dear friend who was a psychologist. He came over when he heard what had happened and asked me if I was taking any antidepressants. When I said no, he wrote me a prescription right then and there."

Grandma told me she never stopped taking them. She said it was possible that the chemicals in my brain were perpetually somewhat unbalanced, regardless of the current traumatic situation, and that antidepressants could become a lifelong regimen for me as well. Because as it turns out, depression runs in my mom's side of the family. It might also run in my dad's side, because I know he struggled with it his entire life.

Antidepressants, my therapist explained, don't actually alter your personality or rob you of your feelings. They do manage the emotional pain so it becomes tolerable, and you can process your feelings without getting overwhelmed. Upon hearing this, I was a lot less apprehensive, and went to the doctor for my first prescription.

Treating depression with medication is a process of trial and error. The first drug may not be strong enough, or it may cause intolerable side effects. I was lucky in that regard, but it took several weeks before the antidepressants began to work. After a while the efficacy would diminish, and the dosage had to be increased. This, I was told, was normal. The only other time my regimen needed to be modified was when Jenn entered hospice. My depression had worsened, so I asked the doctor to adjust my prescription, which she promptly did.

Sometimes my antidepressants were exceedingly effective, especially once they initially built up in my system. I even felt quite happy. Once, on our way to chemotherapy, I said to Jenn, "I'm in a great mood today, and I feel guilty about that." Usually, when we were headed for treatments, my chest was heavy, as I dreaded the side effects Jenn was going to have to endure. My good mood was clearly a result of the antidepressants. Was that okay? Did it make me a bad husband? Jenn said I didn't need to be sad with her, that she would much rather see me happy. It only went on for a week or two, then my emotions tapered down to what I considered normal. What a strange, welcome side effect. Short, but worth it.

I am still on antidepressants now, but am hoping to wean off them eventually. Either way, I know I'll be okay.

My therapist also recommended I take a men's multi-vitamin. I don't know if or how much it contributed to my turnaround or general health, but I started taking it once a day with my antidepressants, and continue to do so.

At some point during my doctor's visit, the issue of sleep came up.

I told her, "I've also been sleeping less. Normally I get at least seven hours, but lately, I've been having trouble falling asleep, and now I'm only getting six hours of sleep a night."

She responded, "The antidepressants might help regulate your sleep cycle, so let's start with that and see what happens. The next time you come in, if you're still having trouble, we can try something else."

That sounded reasonable, and I generally tend to trust experts. During the next month, I experienced anxiety for the first time in my life. A panic attack is a sudden, distressing episode, often with no apparent trigger, and it can be so terrifying, you have to force yourself to breathe. I would then find a quiet place and try to ride it out. This happened almost daily. When I told my doctor at the next visit, she agreed to start me on a low dose of anti-anxiety medication.

I also said, "I'm sleeping less now. Last time I told you I was getting six hours of sleep. Now it's down to five hours, and I'm really starting to worry." I expressed that the lack of sleep made it difficult to function at work and have the energy I needed at home.

She explained, "The medication I'm prescribing for your anxiety will calm you. It slightly slows down your brain, which may help with the insomnia. I'd rather not overdo it, so let's see if this improves your sleep cycle. If not, we can try something else."

Okay, I thought, *I sure hope so, because if this doesn't do it, what's next? Four hours of sleep a night?*

That was exactly right. Another month went by before my next follow up, and I was down to four hours of sleep. I took the anti-anxiety medication for a couple of weeks, until I experienced strange side effects. It did make me sleepy, but also caused an intense tingling sensation in my extremities, and my heart was racing. After a few days the drowsiness stopped, though the tingling interfered with my ability to walk, and the heart palpitations were unsettling. So, I quit taking it.

The sleep deprivation made me feel like a zombie. Getting out of bed in the morning was an enormous struggle. Every day at work I was walking around in a daze. I have no idea how I managed to function at all, or didn't doze off at the wheel while driving the boys and myself to therapy, an hour and a half away. It was normal for me to fall asleep in the living room recliner right after dinner. I would wake up with enough energy to get the kids through their night time routine, but later struggle to go back to sleep. Then the cycle would repeat, only with me feeling a little worse than the day before.

I explained all this to my doctor, "The first time I came to see you, I was getting six hours of sleep a night. A month later it was five, and now I'm down to *four* hours. Isn't there anything we can do? I can barely function, and I *really* think some kind of sleep aid would be beneficial."

"Sure." she said, "Plus, sleeping more could help with your anxiety. You'll handle stress better if you're getting a full night's rest." Then she wrote me a prescription for a sedative.

Finally. I don't want to give you the wrong impression, my doctor is great, and she listens. She was the one at the clinic who detected Jenn's tumor, and fast-tracked her at the imaging center. I trusted her. But I was just so exhausted.

Getting enough sleep was life-altering. I had more energy, less stress, was able to perform better at work and at home, even the panic attacks went away. My entire outlook improved.

Seeking help and taking medication, when you're not strong enough on your own is *not* a sign of weakness. It is, I believe, a sign of even greater strength. My family needed me, and I did whatever it took to be there for them.

My therapist encouraged me to lean on my friends more. I had only been calling them, or my dad, whenever I felt I was about to burst. She said it was important to make it a habit, so that night I posted on Facebook.

"Okay, I can't do this by myself anymore. I need friends I can call and talk to. Would any of you be available? Please only respond if you are willing to listen to me talk about some really dark and depressing stuff."

Many of my old friends got in contact, offering to let me vent to them. I was grateful, and made a list of the people I felt most comfortable with, and the times they'd be around. Then I memorized their schedules, and pretty soon I knew who was available during the day, the evening, and whom I could call in the middle of the night, if I needed to.

I did not speak to friends as regularly as I would have liked, finding the time was a real challenge. Still, being able to call someone was better than nothing. And when I talked to them, it did help.

I didn't always want to discuss what I was dealing with. I avoided conversations about the tough stuff, because it was already on my mind all the time. What frequently happened though, is that a chat about video games, teaching band, or the Dallas Cowboys, would allow me to open up, and be more comfortable talking about the difficult issues.

On one occasion I called my friend Jason. I was crying, and struggling to speak. "Are you okay?" he asked, concerned.

Through tears, I said, "I feel like I need to talk to someone... but I don't even know what to say."

He replied, "That's okay. Let's just chat about anything... Did I tell you that I bought a saxophone?"

It was the start of a good conversation which moved from music to games, and eventually led to my problems. Jason handled the situation perfectly. I literally couldn't speak, even though I wanted to, so he took the lead until I was able to talk about what was bothering me.

I was also extremely fortunate to have a grief mentor. A grief mentor is anyone who previously went through what you're going through, or at least a scenario similar enough so they can relate, and support you along the way. Ideally, it is somebody already beyond their grief.

Angel came into my life after Jenn was diagnosed with the recurrence. Not only is he an incredibly kind, calm, and cool person, he is also the owner and chef of the best restaurant in town. Several people had told me I should talk to him, that he had lost his first wife to a terminal illness. I just couldn't find the courage to approach him.

Then, I had a huge breakthrough, in which he played a major role. It was a therapy day, and my mom had taken the boys out for lunch and playtime, while I went to my appointment. In the session, we must have talked about the future, how I would handle everything, and what I needed to do to be prepared. Topics I usually tried to stay far, far away from.

Afterward, I sat in one of their massage chairs, watching YouTube videos. There was this guru for all things self-help, motivation and inspiration, who had amassed an impressive community, and a video popped up, "Signs Your Heartbreak is OVER!" It was set in the context of a typical boyfriend/girlfriend relationship, but heartbreak is heartbreak. I can't even remember what he said exactly, but I felt inspired and had a breakdown, because he clearly conveyed this message of, "It's going to be okay." It helped me envision what healing could look like, and, for the first time, I was able to picture a future in which things might actually be okay again.

That evening was our traditional family night. I ordered pizza, and while waiting for the call to let us know it was ready for pickup, we started watching The Flash. In this episode, The Flash was stuck in the Speed Force, manifested as an alternate dimension, and the Speed Force was showing him important places, his family and friends, all while trying to help him deal with his mother's death. Flash's journey toward acceptance was so touching, it deeply affected me, and it had an impact on the boys as well.

Halfway through the episode, Angel showed up at our house, delivering the pizza in person. They don't usually do that, but he felt bad, because the order had taken so long. When I tried to pay him, he refused, and told us to enjoy our time together as a family.

As he was about to leave, I thought to myself: *This is your chance. Say something!*

"Hey Angel," I started, "I've heard that you've been through what I'm going through now." He nodded, looking sad. "I've been meaning to come up and talk to you this entire past year, but somehow never did. I probably didn't want to be a bother.

But honestly, I could really use your advice. It seems like you and your family are so happy and doing well. I would love hearing about your experience, how you managed to get there. May I come by to visit with you sometime?"

Angel looked torn, and I knew why. His restaurant was still open, and they needed him in the kitchen. But, he also wanted to talk to me, if only for a few minutes. He chose to stay, and we had a deep and much-needed conversation.

He and his first wife were enjoying life in one of the major cities in Texas. While he was working his dream job, his wife worked at his other dream job – a golf course. They had a beautiful son together, and were financially well-off. Then her illness hit. It wasn't cancer, but the effects were equally devastating.

Besides the obvious emotional trauma they endured, all the money they had, including their entire savings, was spent on medical bills. This was before the Affordable Care Act and the Healthcare Bill of Rights were passed into law during the Obama Administration. Maximum out of pocket protections did not exist, and insurance companies had lifetime limits of what they were required to pay. They quickly hit that limit, after which they were financially and emotionally ruined.

After his wife died, it took him about two years to recover. He said he wasted a lot of time feeling angry. "Eventually I realized, it's just life, you know? What can you do?" *Nothing* was the obvious answer. A simple statement, yet it had a profound impact. Repeating it to myself helped me deal with my own anger issues. *It's just life. What can you do?*

73

Those two years were a long, tough road for him and his son. Even when he met his current wife – after he dated a few other women, who didn't quite understand his situation as a widower and single dad, it wasn't easy. But they figured it out, made it work, and now live as one happy family.

Jenn came outside for the second half of the conversation, and was also deeply touched. Angel's story gave us hope that the boys and I would eventually be okay, even if it took a while. Just as my grandma had demonstrated, it was possible to move on with life. Everything was going to be okay. That sentiment kept coming up. After this meaningful exchange, we went inside to eat pizza and finish watching The Flash.

The climax of the episode sees Barry Allen back at his childhood home, where the Speed Force is presenting itself as his mother. He sits down, and relishes the opportunity to feel her love one last time. His mom begins to read a children's book about the love a mother dinosaur has for her baby dinosaur, and a few pages in, Barry Allen recites the story from memory. He then has one final conversation with his mom, before being offered the chance to leave the Speed Force, so he can help his friends, which he does just in the nick of time. In the end, Barry appears more at ease than ever, and, despite the overwhelming odds against the season's main villain, he assures his team that everything is going to be okay. After hearing the message for the third time that day, it truly connected. I felt it. Everything was going to be okay.

Angel decided to help us out with food. Knowing firsthand how difficult it can be to feed your family during a health crisis, he told us we were welcome to eat at his restaurant anytime, on him. We made sure not to take advantage, but it was immensely helpful for quite a while, until I was ready to cook dinner most nights of the week.

Angel wasn't the only one feeding us. The local churches ran a program, cooking for families in need. We ended up on their list, so they started bringing dinner two or three times a week, every week, for several months. Amazing. I will never forget that.

See if you can find a grief mentor, even if their story isn't exactly the same as yours. They understand you on a deeper level, and may provide you with a glimmer of hope in the darkness of depression. They are living proof that you won't be grieving forever, that one day, you will find happiness again. Perhaps you might even get the chance to share your experience, by being a grief mentor for someone else.

My daily routine became very important. Misty explained I would need something to hang on to once my wife was dead, and having a firm schedule would allow me to go into auto-pilot, so I could continue getting things done, while not expending the mental energy I needed to process what was happening. So, in preparation for my worst nightmare, I began building a solid routine. One small thing at a time.

Luckily, I already had a nighttime ritual with my kids. Our typical evening involves eating dinner at six o'clock. By seven, Kayden has to get in the bath. Devin will take his bath sometime between seven thirty and eight o'clock, while Kayden is getting dried off and dressed. After Kayden is done, he'll bring me his toothbrush so we can brush his teeth, and about that time Devin will be getting out of the bath. I have read to my kids or had them read to themselves, almost every night of their life. Kayden's story time is at eight fifteen and bedtime at eight thirty. Before he gets into bed, he'll tell everyone goodnight and give hugs, and maybe even kisses depending on who you are. Then I tuck him in. That's when Devin's story time starts. At eight fifty, Devin and I have "hang out time", where we sit and talk about whatever is on our mind. Sometimes big questions come up. Often it's just small stuff. At nine o'clock I tuck Devin in. When I put the boys into bed at night, I always tell them six things, "I love you. I'm proud of you. You are a great son, and you're a great brother. Sweet dreams. Good night!" They usually say those things back to me, which is cute and warms my heart. I love my boys.

Before six o'clock though, I had a couple of unstructured hours, and more time after the boys were asleep. This still gave me a solid foundation to build off of. My next task was to learn cooking. I didn't add that to the routine until the summer of 2016, when I began trying to make dinner every other night, at least three nights per week, until I was up to five nights. I studied by watching instructional cooking videos on YouTube, before getting started. Soon I was developing a decent level of proficiency.

Listening to music was another way to boost my endorphins, according to my therapist. I've always been a music lover, and listen to a wide range from classical to rock, rap, anime soundtracks, and everything in between. But as my passion for music faded, so did my habit of listening to it regularly. At that point, I was only turning on music in the car, and that never lasted for long, unless I was on the road.

Misty recommended I start listening to music whenever possible. "Just incorporate it into everything you do," she said. Now I put on my playlist while I cook, fold laundry, clean the house, mow the yard, play Minecraft, and of course on the road. Whenever I was alone in the car, I sang my heart out for the entire hour and a half drive, releasing a lot of pent-up emotion. Even if I'm cooking in the kitchen, I've come out of my shell enough that I'll sing along to the songs with appropriate language. I even dance and head-bang for that extra kick of fun.

Music not only releases endorphins, but it can also be highly therapeutic. I found myself connecting to and understanding lyrics I could never relate to before. In particular Coheed and Cambria's album "The Color Before the Sun", and a couple of tracks from their other records. But that album has some songs that fit Jenn's and my emotions perfectly, like the lyrics from *Here to Mars*. Claudio Sanchez talks about how no one in the universe could replace his beloved, which is driving him into a dark place, and how much it hurts to be in a world without her.

Another song I cried to is called *Pearl of the Stars*. In it, he sings about his loved one dying, and references a baby girl he'll one-day share stories of his beloved with, how amazing she was, and how much she meant to him. Thinking of having to tell the boys about their mom when they get older made me sad.

There are some lines describing Jenn pretty well in a song called *Colors*, where Sanchez again sings about depression and losing a loved one. He describes himself as tired and opaque, and gives you a sense of the fog despair brings. He goes on about memories of when life was good, how he'll never get that life back, and feels as if he's lost himself. He mentions his loved one having many scars. All of this brought me to tears every time I listened, and the chorus made me both dread and wonder what the moment of Jenn's passing would feel like. Sanchez advises being still and quiet and just letting it happen. He asks the listener, as they are in that still and quiet moment, does it feel good to let go? Would Jenn's moment of death feel like this?

Then there was hard rock, when I needed to crank my energy up, like Twelve Foot Ninja. Their latest album, *Outlier,* has a couple of songs Jenn and I jammed out to constantly. *Invincible* is incredible. The first part relates to Jenn's sense of denial and self-doubt, while the next couple of lines express our reaction to the news that the cancer had returned. We knew there was a strong chance of a reoccurrence, but we chose to believe she would beat it. In that sense, we were fools, but there's wisdom in taking that approach as well. The highs referenced describe her feeling overwhelmed by the love and support from the local community, online through her YouTube channel and Facebook page, and all of the donations we received, which let us cross off items from her bucket list. The lows are self-explanatory. In the build-up to the climax, the lyrics describe fighting a mountain, and just when you think you reached the top, you find there's another mountain blotting out the sun. This is what Jenn felt like, being diagnosed with a reoccurrence after thinking she had beaten her cancer.

Dave Matthews Band has a couple of songs that gave me the inspiration and courage to continue pushing through. The lyrics in the song *Sweet* made me hopeful. Matthews sings about the struggle to swim and keep your head above water, encouraging you to never give up, and reminding you of how sweet it feels to get to the other side. It put some light down at the end of my dark tunnel.

These songs, among others, became the soundtrack to my grief journey.

Being depressed is not a laughing matter, but finding something to laugh at was another assignment from Misty.

I discovered two diversions that were always good for a chuckle. One a parody metal band, the other an anime podcast. Both were filled with obscenely vulgar language, and crude, sexual humor of the kind I would never use myself, but that's probably part of why I enjoy it so much.

I tried to find entertaining YouTube creators. Most of what I watch are "Let's Play" videos, where someone is playing a game and giving commentary as they go. I was looking for creators who seemed to love what they do, and went all out for their audiences. YouTube, in general, has a vast community of artists, many of whom have a great sense of humor. And it's free. Kayden's biggest interest was and continues to be funny cat videos.

The final item on Misty's list of ideas to boost endorphins was physical activity. Well, not exactly. The last task on the agenda was sex, which was completely out of my control. So physical activity of any kind had to do. The problem was, it's always difficult to motivate yourself to exercise, let alone when you're depressed. I bought a work out bench and didn't assemble it for several months. But I started doing more chores. Lawn care was the surprising winner. I had gotten tired of the sad state of our yard, and wondered how nice I could make it look if I applied myself.

Once I decided to tackle the yard, I went to YouTube and started watching lawn care videos. Then I ordered several new toys from Amazon, and got to work. I put on those boards with spikes attached to your shoes, and walked around the yard to loosen the soil and prepare it for seeding and feeding. Weed treatment was next, followed by tossing seed, distributing fertilizer, and so on. Not only did I mow, but I had purchased my first weed eater, to trim around the house and various objects in our yard. Among my new gadgets was an edger to fix the sidewalks, and a striper I sadly never used.

For a few months, until the cold season arrived, I was outside one to three times a week doing yard work and maintenance. I got a bit discouraged when the weeds didn't completely die off, and the grass didn't grow, although it did develop in the shady areas. Still, the yard looked far better than it ever had. More importantly, I was being active again. After jamming out to music and doing yard work for an hour, I felt substantially better.

Therapy was critical in my journey through the depths of my despair. Misty pointed me to the light, and then showed me how to walk toward it. It was a long path, requiring a lot of compassion for myself, when I couldn't finish tasks or failed to follow Misty's recommendations. Eventually, I got better at it, but it's still a work in progress.

After five or six months of therapy, my mental health had improved remarkably. It was a combination of antidepressants, getting enough sleep, and incorporating good habits to keep the endorphin levels up and me busy. Now I was able to shoulder not only my burdens, but those of Jenn and the boys', and help them deal with their grief as well. Thanks to my therapist, my physician, and the numerous baby steps I took over the course of these months, I found my strength at the time when my family needed me the most.

Chapter 4

Caretaking

*"Remember that in the long run you will benefit from caregiving...
because you will have no regrets knowing that you did what you could
and what was right."*

– GAIL L.

CANCER, JUST AS any other serious illness or life-threatening condition, is like a meteor strike. The patient in the center takes the worst hit, but it affects everyone around them. Whenever Jenn lamented the amount of pain and grief her illness was causing me, the boys, her parents and friends, I always told her, "Yes, but it's harder on you than anyone else. At least we get to live." Being a caretaker is difficult, often overwhelmingly so, but it is important, even helpful, to remember it is the patient who ultimately suffers most.

When Jenn was initially diagnosed, one of the first people I went to was her step-dad, Charles. I asked how he helped Cindy, Jenn's mother. "Oh, Jenn will get you through this nice and easy," he answered.

"I don't doubt that," I said, "but how do I help *her* make it through?"

He said I should keep Jenn on her toes, explaining that he would playfully pick on Cindy, to get her to snap out of the dark moods. Mind you, I had been tormented throughout grade school until my junior year of high school, so ribbing always felt too close to bullying to me. I didn't like it, and had no practice.

But it was highly effective with my wife. Jenn herself was quite the jokester and loved pranks. So as long as she saw me smiling, she understood I was kidding. It helped her come back from whatever dark place she had been in, to the present, where she could enjoy life as it was right now, instead of dreading an uncertain future. There is a way to turn even the worst moments into something funny. Laughter, as they say, is the best medicine. At least for the spirit.

Cancer drastically changed our sense of humor. During the entire time, but especially after Jenn was diagnosed as stage IV, a lot of it was death-related, or dark humor. Sometimes, our jokes fell flat or made people uncomfortable. You can't help that, but it also brought the two of us closer together, and created strong bonds with patients and caretakers who shared the same dark sense of humor.

Early on, we assured Jenn it was okay not to be okay. I've heard horror stories of men telling their sick spouses to suck it up, not to complain, or be a nuisance. That is an awful approach. I taught my children that people are like balloons, and emotions the air or water. If a balloon fills up too much, it will burst. Similarly, when you keep bottling up your feelings, repressing them, they don't just go away. They continue building up inside of you, until eventually, they all erupt at once in an uncontrolled, violent blast, hurting you and those around you.

For me, crying was an essential part of the healing process, and I encouraged Jenn not to hold anything in either, to freely express her emotions as they came. It was okay for her to be frustrated, sad, depressed, angry, bitter. Sometimes that meant extended crying fits, swearing a lot, even around the boys, or loudly yelling "This sucks! Cancer fucking sucks!"

She needed the space to process those feelings, so she could get back to enjoying the life she had left.

We tried our best to help Jenn focus on the positive, to make the tough days more bearable by filling them with activities she still enjoyed. You do what you can to distract the patient from however awful the current circumstances may be.

This meant giving Jenn permanent control over the car radio. Most road trips were either going to, or returning from treatments and consultations. If listening to her favorite music could make these journeys just a little more fun, it was worth it. Jenn basically got to do whatever she wanted. For example, she was an avid consumer, and loved shopping. Early on, there were only occasional purchases using donated money, but once she started receiving social security checks for her disability – be sure to inform yourself of any benefits you may be entitled to, she was able to spend more freely.

Jenn did feel conflicted about that. Part of her thought she should be saving some of it for when she would be gone, to leave more behind for us. She also wanted to put the money aside for the boys' college education, or other equally responsible purposes.

I told Jenn not to worry about it. As long as we were able to pay our regular bills, including the substantial monthly payments to doctors and hospitals, it was fine for her to spend money on whatever she desired. Be it stuff to make her more comfortable, donating to a cause she felt strongly about, or investing in equipment for her YouTube videos and other social media endeavors, I didn't care. She loved buying extravagant gifts for the boys, like a trampoline for Kayden's room, or me, like a powerful new gaming laptop, after my old one had died.

I said to Jenn, "You are dying. Do whatever you want. If spending money helps you feel better, even just a little bit, then go for it. I will sort out the financial stuff after you're gone. Leave it to me."

This led to certain larger impulse purchases, like five VIP tickets to see Pentatonix, with access to the sound check and a meet and greet. Was it expensive? Sure. Was it worth it? Absolutely. Life is short enough for all of us, but Jenn's especially so. We needed to pack as much enjoyment into it as possible.

Even allowing her to take this ostensibly irresponsible approach to money, I have since managed to sort out the finances, fulfilling my promise. It worked out fine, and I have zero regrets.

During the cancer journey, Jenn often felt alone, especially at first. So we did what we could to let her know there was always someone by her side, every single step of the way.

Making her medical appointments a priority was very important. I am not sure exactly how many days of work I missed over those two and a half years, but it was a lot. My principal and superintendent were so supportive, I can never thank them enough.

"Look, Coop," the principal said, using his hands to indicate the levels of importance, "God, family, then work."

The superintendent put it like this, "You do whatever you need to, to take care of your family. We'll take care of the rest."

I am also forever grateful to Adrian for covering my classes when I had to be with Jenn. But it took more than just these three. I previously mentioned how coworkers had donated some of their personal days, so I could use those instead of losing income. On top of that, my absence regularly interfered with other school business, and I assume everyone on the faculty must have been inconvenienced at some point in time. They were all so gracious and understanding, which significantly reduced the pressure I felt, allowing me to focus on Jenn's needs. I wish everyone dealing with a crisis of this magnitude could have that kind of uncompromising support at work.

Consequently, I was able to accompany Jenn to almost all consultations, surgeries, and treatments. Toward the end, there were a few appointments I had to miss, because the time constraints had gotten worse, and I was juggling a lot at once.

Jenn was fortunate to have amazing friends, who were happy to take her to chemo or radiation therapy on the rare occasion when I could not.

Someone always had to drive her, because the Benadryl, given to prevent an allergic reaction, made her very drowsy. Even if Jenn took a nap, after chemo there was only a brief window of time, when she would be awake and able to eat or run an errand. As treatment wore on, this window decreased from a few hours to as little as thirty minutes. I was thankful for anybody covering the routine trips, so I could make sure to attend all the consultations. Those were crucial, because that's when her doctor informed us of positive or negative test results, and any consequential changes in the treatment plan.

My being there meant a lot to Jenn. She knew how important work was to me, and the fact that I was giving up time with my students to be by her side, made her feel that much more special. There were times when she wanted to cancel appointments, fearful of the terrible side effects. I understood completely, and told her it was okay to not go, but I think my presence then served as a reminder that she was going through this hell for her family, and that gave her the courage to persevere.

There are many items that can make a cancer patient – or any other gravely ill person – more comfortable. For about the first year of treatment, most of Jenn's discomfort was caused by side effects. Our goal was to find ways to counteract them.

Jenn did a lot of research, and whenever she discovered something interesting, like Jeans Cream for radiation burns, she would either order it online, or send me to a store. If we couldn't find it in our small town, Cindy or a friend rushed to bring it from San Angelo. You just want to get your loved one the relief they need, and fast. We learned it's best to figure out the side effects of any new treatment regimen ahead of time, to be prepared.

After chemo, Jenn had to deal with an intense sensitivity to light, which often led to migraines. We had to have sunglasses in the car at all times, and the bigger the shades, the better. If you look at older pictures of Jenn on Facebook, she was always wearing gigantic sunglasses, and that was the reason. We also got her eye masks for the "chemo bag" and her bedside. When she was feeling sleepy, or getting irritated by too much brightness – especially in the chemo room, where we had no control over the lighting, she could just put on her eye mask and nod off.

Other items in the chemo bag included a neck pillow. Jenn's favorite one had a breast on each end of the horseshoe shape. She thought it was hilarious – remember, incorporating humor when possible, and the staff and at least some of the other patients did, too. Jenn carried chapstick at all times, because her lips and mouth were continuously painfully dry. Lots of water and ice helped moisten the mouth, but only lip balm or vaseline improved the chapped lips.

Jenn was always uncomfortably cold while receiving chemotherapy. They must have stored the drugs in a fridge or freezer, because as soon as the IV drip started, she could feel the icy liquid coursing through her veins. We did anything to keep her warm, outfitting her as if for an arctic expedition – in Texas, mind you. This included a thick blanket, gloves, a second pair of socks and snow boots.

Of course we brought numerous electronic devices, to entertain Jenn as long as she was awake. I packed her laptop, though she usually preferred just the iPod. However, most of the time her mom or friends came to visit, so she focused on them, and didn't need a digital distraction. Being surrounded by loved ones during chemotherapy makes a big difference.

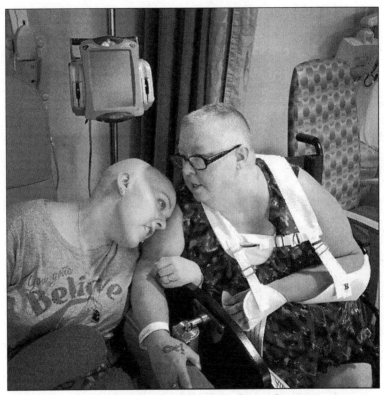

Jenn with her mom during chemotherapy.

We did have to carefully manage the number of people visiting at the same time, as there are limits, set by the hospital. Generally we tried to keep it down to myself plus two additional visitors – one of them often her mom, and the staff seemed happy with that. Most of the patients had nobody, which was quite sad. I know I would not want to be alone while poison is running through my veins.

Once we settled in, I was mostly playing Minecraft, to not have to think about Jenn being pumped full of stuff, that would later make her feel like death. But, I was also always happy to get whatever was needed, anything really. I was the one to jump at the chance to pick up coffee, water, or snacks. Having a purpose is distracting in its own way. If we happened to be there around lunchtime, I would bring in meals. Starbucks cups were omnipresent, as all of us could use the caffeine.

After treatment care was equally important. Jenn needed her blanket and extra layers of clothing on the way home, as well as copious amounts of tissues for her post chemo runny nose. If she was hungry, we went to one of her favorite places, so she could eat before passing out.

When we initially learned that chemotherapy would cause Jenn to lose all her hair, she was devastated. As a sign of solidarity, I shaved my head first. We asked the boys if they wanted to go bald with us, but they declined. Then Devin managed to get a hold of the dog clippers, and, while playing around, accidentally took some of his own hair out. He didn't have to go completely bald, but close enough for some good family pictures.

Kayden, myself, Jenn and Devin. Devin wasn't bald, yet, but I was.

As a caretaker, I was prepared to act as Jenn's nurse and butler. Everyone expects that, but it doesn't make it any less tiring. I did my best to balance being available to her, taking care of the kids, work, the house and myself.

While Jenn was recovering from chemo, she didn't need much. She mostly slept, and was self-sufficient during the day, when I was at work. But as her health deteriorated, her strength was waning, and dinner became my responsibility. I, however, being too depressed and unmotivated to cook, would just run out and pick up some type of fast food. Eventually, though, I did learn how to prepare healthy meals for the family. Anything Jenn needed, such as drinks, snacks or medication, I brought to her bedside. At one point we even set up a bell, so she could assume the role of rich, spoiled madam, ringing for the manservant to rush to her aid – that scenario made us laugh so many times, despite the otherwise bleak situation.

Then there are the more delicate nurse duties. Most of it wasn't dramatic, but during the post surgery and hospice care it helped to have a strong stomach. For example, after Jenn's skin-sparing, double mastectomy, she had tubes running out of each pocket of leftover skin, into bags collecting fluid. To prevent a potentially life-threatening infection, it was critical to empty these bags as necessary. It also meant manually squeezing all the liquid through the tubes, since they needed to be cleaned out regularly. Then we had to meticulously document how much fluid was collected and discarded.

You're wearing gloves during this procedure, but it's still disgusting. In hindsight, the gross stuff wasn't as difficult to handle as I had expected. Jenn depended on me, and it was as if my stomach knew that. Instinctively, I was able to do what needed to be done.

I could list many more instances, but I think you get the idea, so I'll spare you the details. We just did what had to be done to take care of Jenn, and make her treatment as bearable as possible.

Chapter 5

Sharing the Journey

"Check your boobs. Check your balls. And when life gets overwhelming, just think, this too shall pass."

– JENNY COOPER

JENN LOVED WATCHING makeup tutorials, animal rescues, vlogs, etcetera on YouTube. She herself uploaded short videos of the children regularly, so the grandparents, living in other parts of Texas and Canada, could see the boys in action.

Jenn first experimented with creating a vlog style video after she had joined Fitocracy and started losing weight. Members of the Fito community tagged each other to post a short film answering questions about themselves. You can still find Jenn's if you search far enough back. Her sense of humor comes through, but you can tell she's feeling shy.

A few videos later, Jenn began dreaming about turning her YouTube channel into a vlog page. She didn't quite post regularly, but often discovered fun ideas from other vloggers, and enjoyed making similar videos with her friends.

When Jenn was diagnosed with cancer, she turned to YouTube. She was looking for other women with cancer, to learn more about it, but I think mostly to ease her fears. In the process, she found a couple of women battling breast cancer, who were documenting their journeys on YouTube. She quickly fell in love with them. One was diagnosed as a young adult, the other had a lovely family, and they all shared a beautiful spirit.

What they were doing inspired Jenn to share her journey as well. I know she wanted to help others going through treatment, by giving them someone to relate to, and also to educate women the way she had learned from other cancer vloggers.

Soon after, she started a Facebook page called Coopdizzle – the name of her YouTube channel and Twitter account, where she shared her thoughts, emotions, and cancer updates on a regular basis. Jenn often wrote about her anxiety and fears, and posted images from scans. After most treatments she made videos, once or twice a month. In both her vlogs and the writings on her page, she was very open and uncensored.

You would have to ask her followers what about Jenn drew people in. People have told me it was her humor, charm, beautiful spirit, and honesty, as well as the fact that she had a loving family, suffering by her side. Many of her subscribers were fellow breast cancer patients, some survivors, but other people from all over the world and all walks of life ended up finding Jenn.

About six months into her social media endeavors, in early September, she had her first TV appearance on one of the local stations in San Angelo. I remember it being a short, but beautiful interview feature, and Jenn was terrific in it. Especially considering what else had happened.

The day of the interview – approximately a week or two before the broadcast, her mom Cindy was taking care of Jenn and the boys after a chemotherapy treatment. She was feeling exhausted that afternoon. Her speech was slurry, which caught my attention, but Cindy insisted she just needed to take a nap. In the meantime, the reporter and cameraman were getting everything set up for the interview. When Cindy returned, her face looked a little droopy, the speech was worse, and she couldn't walk straight. I recognized these were signs of a stroke. Cindy reiterated she just needed more rest, but now we demanded that she see a doctor. We practically forced her into the car. Jenn was anxious about her mom, who felt terribly guilty worrying her daughter right before the TV interview. The news team even offered to come back another day, but I reassured Jenn I would take good care of Cindy. She could stay for the interview, and meet us at the hospital afterward. Watching the feature, you would have never known Jenn was freaking out inside about her mom possibly having a stroke. She was calm, collected, professional and beautiful.

The hospital was a nightmare. I pulled straight up to the emergency room door, where the ambulance would typically park, and rang their doorbell. Someone answered over an intercom, "Can we help you?"

"Yes, ma'am. I think my mother-in-law is having a stroke. We need some help!" I answered with a sense of urgency.

A team came outside to help get Cindy out of the car, questioning me in a not particularly helpful tone. "What makes you think she's having a stroke?" I listed the symptoms of a stroke, all of which she was presenting with right in front of them. They put her in a bed, and we waited over half an hour for the on-call doctor to show up. As a side note, we live in a town with a population of two thousand people, and it takes less than five minutes to drive from one end to the other. Eventually he came in, as doubtful and dismissive as the staff had been regarding my concerns, and decided to run some tests.

The bullshit – I'm sorry, it still makes me angry – about this is, I later found out, that as soon as I mentioned the word stroke, they were supposed to send Cindy to another hospital. They did not have an MRI machine, which is required to rule out the possibility of a stroke. Had I known that, I would have driven to San Angelo, so she could get the treatment she needed to save her full mental and physical capacity.

Instead, they had Cindy wait for hours in a room while they ran tests. At some point, the doctor returned and declared she was most likely suffering from stress, since her daughter was dealing with breast cancer. By then, all of the symptoms were substantially worse. Jenn's reaction, she told me later, was, "Really? Do you see her? You call that stress?"

To which the doctor responded, "Yes. Symptoms of extreme stress can look like a stroke." He prescribed some medication to help her relax and told her to rest. So, Cindy was picked up by her husband, went home, took the pills, and proceeded to have numerous mini-strokes throughout the night. By the time her husband drove her to the hospital in San Angelo, substantial and irreparable damage had already been done. This was when we realized that the first doctor had committed malpractice, and several of the staff gladly agreed to testify to that effect.

We really wanted to sue the idiot, but didn't have the money to hire an attorney. Cindy required several months of physical and speech therapy, just to be able to do some things on her own again. The stroke was a devastating blow to our family. Cindy had been a huge help after Jenn's treatments, and now she needed help herself, but more importantly, her personality was never quite the same after. At least that doctor is retired now.

However, soon after Jenn's segment aired, she was interviewed by the San Angelo Standard Times. Both the TV segment and the newspaper article attracted additional YouTube subscribers and Facebook/Twitter followers.

Jenn had other newspaper features. At least two more after the first. She was also on a local news station in the Midland/Odessa area. One of the articles was picked up in other cities in Texas, and we only found out through her social media followers. Each event resulted in a spike in subscribers and followers. She was blowing up. As was her message and cause.

Jenn was invited to participate in different events, one of them a free painting class for selected breast cancer patients. I don't think she was chosen because of her public profile, as none of the other participants were as open with their cancer, but she enjoyed going to the classes and painting. The catch was that the San Angelo Fine Arts Museum was putting on an exhibit, throwing a party for its launch, featuring the women and their art.

Jenn created two paintings. On a black background, she drew the Metavivor ribbon, which represents metastatic breast cancer and has three colors: pink, light blue, and light green. The other was my favorite, not just of hers, but the entire exhibit. A black and purple spiral, at the center a concentrated roundish shape. It symbolizes the cancer and Jenn's mental anguish surrounding it. Her mom has the first painting, but I kept this one and it's still on display in our house.

Jenn next to one of her paintings at the exhibit.

It was a formal event, and Jenn was introduced onstage in front of a large crowd, her story featured in both the program and a placard below her paintings.

She was honored to have been offered the opportunity to speak at an event for the Laura W. Bush Institute for Women's Health in San Angelo. It was hosted at the local library and also quite formal. Jenn was the opening act for another speaker. She may have seemed a bit out of her element for someone who had made so many videos and appearances in the news, yet she handled herself really well and gave a great speech. I only wish I had a video or transcript, to preserve it for the boys.

Jenn was interviewed and featured in an online magazine called The Underbelly, which covers, "the dark side of breast cancer." I believe it was this article, about Death With Dignity, that got picked up by a few other magazines, including Good Housekeeping and the Cosmopolitan. Jenn was so excited about landing in a nationwide publication, we were incredibly proud of her. By this time, she had garnered a couple of thousand subscribers on YouTube and about as many followers on Facebook. Strangers messaged her to share how her article was eye opening for them, and that reading it had changed their stance on compassionate death laws. We knew then, that her message of real education and awareness, rather than the "pink party" image you see in the mainstream media, was making a real impact.

Through all of this, Jenn was contacted to be a spokeswoman for Metavivor. If you want to help metastatic breast cancer patients, please donate. They have been promoted over Susan G. Komen for the Cure by virtually anyone who has done their homework on the practices of Komen. Whereas Susan G. Komen for the Cure spends millions of dollars in salaries for their top officers, but only donates 20% of its budget toward research, less than half of which is for metastatic breast cancer research, Metavivor donates all the money it receives to research, specifically for metastatic breast cancer. These patients are often forgotten in research and funding, because they're viewed as lost causes. To those people, it makes more sense to spend money on education, so cancers are caught before they spread, and to figure out better treatments for early-stage breast cancer, so patients don't reach the metastatic stage. That basically means giving up on patients with MBC, thinking they are as good as dead. I strongly disagree with this approach. Metavivor can give so much, because everyone working for them does so on a volunteer basis, and nearly all volunteers are themselves metastatic breast cancer patients, so they are very devoted to their cause. Jenn was extremely proud of being a spokeswoman for such a wonderful organization. She took it seriously and promoted them with a passion.

Toward the end of Jenn's life, her YouTube channel was nominated for a WEGO Health Award: Best in Show on YouTube and it finished as a finalist. It was incredible how far her reach had become, and the huge amount of people she affected through her tireless efforts.

"Hey guys, this is Jenny, aka Coopdizzle!" This is how she opened all her YouTube videos. Her popular ones have over twenty thousand views.

The most famous video is her goodbye video, simply titled, "I'm Dead =(," with over sixty thousand views. Thoughtfully, Jenn starts by informing everyone that she's passed away, then reflects on her entire cancer journey. To me, the best part is when she starts contemplating what is important in life. She describes how having cancer put things in perspective for her, as far as who and what truly matter. She talks about having to cut dramatic people from her life, including family members – whom she had wanted for years to have a good relationship with – because they were always surrounded by too much drama. I think this is great advice for everyone. Removing people from your life is not easy, but sometimes it's for the best, as was the case for her. Once Jenn realized her life would be significantly shortened, she did not want to waste a minute of the remaining time with unnecessary turmoil. Then she asks her audience, that if they ever happen to see her boys, to please tell them how much she loved them. We hear about a conversation she had with Devin, where she apologized that she will be his first heartbreak, how she instead wanted to be there for him when a girl broke his heart for the first time, and how she talked to him about dealing with heartache. She expresses her desire for me to move on and be loved again, and asks her viewers to either donate to her family or Metavivor.org. The advice to her audience, about living life to the fullest, is "Go to as many concerts as you can." At the end, she talks about her hopes for what might happen after death, like being a ghost able to haunt people, or the possibility of reincarnation, "Who knows what happens to us?"

One of Jenn's other high performing videos is called, "End of life realizations... part 1". It opens, and she's lying on her side, in bed. She describes her difficult day with constant vomiting, before running through a list of life lessons. The first being that you shouldn't place too much emphasis on your looks, because life is short, and you need to love yourself so you can enjoy it. Jenn used to be very critical of how she looked, even after she had lost all that weight. Now, close to death, having regained the weight due to steroids, not being able to recognize herself, she remembers that time, and how foolish it was to be so negative about her body, when she should have focused on enjoying life. I believe one of her big regrets was always being down on herself about her looks, even though her mom, myself and others were telling her how beautiful she was. She cries, "I look back at that and I think, holy crap, I really was pretty!" She says, "I wish I could go back and say, Jenny, don't be so hard on yourself. Enjoy your time. Enjoy your youth... Enjoy it because it's going to get really bad." This message targeted specifically her cousin, who grew up with a mom constantly belittling her, despite being beautiful, a straight-A student, and having many other positive attributes. But it is an incredibly powerful message for her to share with everyone. She builds up her audience, saying if they can't find anything good about themselves, they're at least empathetic and compassionate, two beautiful traits they should give themselves credit for. "Try not to be so hard on yourself. Life is way too short." It's excellent advice, and extraordinarily persuasive, coming from her at that time.

The video Jenn was probably most proud of, is called "Death With Dignity." DeathWithDignity.org reached out and asked her to make a video advocating for Death With Dignity laws. She was hugely honored to be a spokeswoman for that organization. They contacted her, because she had been using her page to promote Death With Dignity laws for some time, and had also talked about it in passing in some of her earlier videos.

Jenn became interested in Death With Dignity out of fear of what dying would be like. She recognized that as the cancer got worse, the pain would get worse. She was terribly afraid of suffering in constant agony, struggling to breathe from the cancers on her diaphragm, losing her memory to the cancer in her brain, suffering from bone pains and other symptoms. That's not how she wanted to die. We live in Texas, where compassionate death laws don't exist. Had it been possible, we would have moved to a state, where she was permitted to die on her own terms. Instead, because of the system in Texas and the moral hang-ups about suicide, Death With Dignity is not an option.

First, let me explain, just in case you're not familiar with the debate, or what Death With Dignity promotes. People against these laws will call it something like, "Doctor assisted suicide." I disagree with the suicide part. Death With Dignity laws do not mean that anybody can just ask their doctor for a pill to end their life. They're geared toward people like Jenn, who have a terminal diagnosis, typically brought on by a painful illness, like cancer or an otherwise debilitating disease. Very few people would qualify for it. It is explicitly to provide another option for those, who would otherwise die a terrible and painful death. These patients are going to die, whether they want to or not. They would just rather not suffer in their final days. There is no choice about whether or not to die. That's not suicide, in my opinion.

In states with compassionate death laws on the books, the requirements to qualify for this option are high. It is a long and involved process. Patients must be screened by multiple professionals, to ensure they are of sound mind when making the decision. To explain, if they had come to Jenn when her cancer had taken her memory, even if it were during a moment of clarity, she wouldn't have qualified, although she was in a tremendous amount of fear and pain. As mentioned earlier, they must have certain qualifying illnesses, which are well documented. You have to make multiple oral and written requests, be able to self-administer the medication, and all of these requirements have to be verified by two separate physicians. In addition, you must be at least eighteen years old, and prove residency in your state. In other words, the medication is difficult and time-consuming to obtain, so it's not as if depressed people can quickly gain access to it. They cannot.

Personally, I think it's terrible that this isn't an option everywhere. People in power as well as ordinary folks are typically against it, because they don't agree with suicide. They say a person's death should be between them and their creator. I disagree with it even being suicide under standard terms, and I find it contemptible to take that decision away from an individual, particularly in the "Land of the Free," based on one's individual religious views, which that person may or may not share. Furthermore, Christianity along with most other religions I know of, promote compassion. To me, it's terribly un-compassionate to force someone to die a slow, agonizing, torturous, painful death over the course of several days or multiple weeks. Part of me wants to be understanding of their different world views, which I always respect, but the other part of me wants to say, "What kind of person are you, that you would force someone to suffer like that?" In Texas, and in most other states where Death With Dignity is not an option, it seems we have more compassion for wounded animals than for dying cancer patients. We don't force animals to suffer. Shouldn't terminally ill humans be shown the same level of compassion as a mortally wounded animal?

I think so. I hope that if you disagree, you will at least reconsider. If you still can't come over to this side, I hope you'll at least take the stance of, "I disagree with it, I wouldn't do it myself, but it's not for me to tell someone else what they are or are not allowed to do, with regards to how they would like to die in that situation." This latter position is, in my opinion, the ultimate form of agreeing to disagree, while still being respectful of the other person and their way of life.

Jenn starts her video by asking for understanding, and to withhold judgment before launching into some background about her case, the history of her treatment, when her remission happened, and the several locations of cancer within her body. I think she was trying to make it clear that she didn't choose this, that cancer can be very aggressive, and that you can only do so much to fight it whether you like it or not.

"I do not want to die. I am thirty-three years old," she says, "I now am married to a wonderful man, who is very respectful, and loves me." Through tears, she goes into the background of her poor relationships with men, and how much our marriage means to her. "We have two beautiful boys. They are four and eight." She shares a heartbreaking detail of a regular back and forth she has with Kayden where she says, "I will love you, always and forever."

Kayden would get teary-eyed and say, "Even when you're dead?"

"Yes, even when I'm dead." She then goes into details about her old life with her first husband, when she was so alone and miserable, she tried to kill herself. She compares that life to the one she has now. "Some people tell me – be positive. I am very positive. I am in love with my family. I have great friends. I have a wonderful support system. But it doesn't change the fact that... I have cancer... and I'm running out of options. So... I don't want to die." She fights through tears to talk about how she wants to see her children grow up, teach them to drive, be there for their first heartbreak, when they go off to college, get married, when they have children. She says she thinks she would be a wonderful grandmother (and she would've been... the best). "And the reality is that I won't... just with breast cancer... forty thousand men and women die every year... That's us, in our thirties, and twenties. And we have babies and children to raise... and not enough is being done for research." After she collects herself, she says very firmly, "I know what my fate is." It is an emotional punch to the gut that shatters your idea of "assisted suicide." How can it be suicide when this person doesn't want to die?

"I'm not afraid to die, either." She starts to talk about all the good things that will happen when she dies, naming off one painful symptom after another, and notes they will come to an end after her many months of suffering. "The only part about dying that kills me emotionally is leaving my husband and my children and my loved ones behind."

"With cancer, you either go really fast or really slow... if I happen to go really slow, the idea of sitting around, hooked up to machines, becoming thin... all of these things and my children seeing that, I feel like that would do more emotional damage to my family than if I were to... gather everybody around, say goodbye and tell them that I love them and that I'm so going to miss them. Taking a drink, and peacefully falling asleep while my kids are peacefully asleep in bed, in the arms of my husband... Everybody wants to die in the arms of their lover. What if I'm too frail to do that, or I'm so out of my mind from my brain mets that I don't know who my children are, or my husband is? That's a horrible thought! That would be more traumatic. If my boys walked into the room and I didn't know who they were because mommy's cancer has eaten her brain up." Through more tears, she continues to argue that to take a drink and, "just go," would be far less traumatic, far more peaceful, than to suffer from pain and lose her mind and memory of her loved ones, and for us to all witness that. And we'll talk more about that later, but she was absolutely right.

After taking a moment to collect herself, she starts to educate her audience on the demanding requirements one must go through just to have that option. "I don't think approving something like Death With Dignity would endanger people... It's not fair to just assume the worst and leave people like me and other people just... suffering. Because that's what you're doing. I don't think it's suicide. I was suicidal once... I actively tried to kill myself... And there was nothing medically wrong with me. Me wanting this option is completely different than me feeling suicidal because I actually want to live, and I have so much to live for. This is me saying... I'm tired. Not right now, but I'll get there. And it makes me really sad to think that when I get there that I won't have this choice." She encourages people to put themselves in her shoes. What would it be like to struggle to breathe? "I don't want to watch my children suffer because they're four and they're eight."

"I don't think that God would be mad at me. Because I honestly feel like the only thing that's holding Death With Dignity back is religion. I don't think that I would be punished for ending my suffering. It's really hard to stay alive when you have cancer that's just going crazy in your body." She ends by asking people to please be kind to her if they have different opinions and says it should be okay to have different views, but you have to be able to have a conversation.

As I read through this chapter, I feel like her words require minimal commentary. She does such an incredible, even masterful job of pleading her case. It was one of the most emotional, and persuasive arguments she ever made.

Her video went viral among the cancer community. She was contacted by multiple high school students, asking to use her video as reference for their school research projects. It was featured on the DeathWithDignity.org website, and no doubt it has made thousands of people question the way they see these laws.

Jenn didn't just use her YouTube videos for self-promotion. She was doing it for a cause. She used it to help people and to make a positive impact on the world. I was so proud of her for all her YouTube work, and I honestly wasn't too surprised that she was gaining such an audience. When I met Jenn and saw her personality, I knew she was a rock star. It's just that nobody seemed to see it, including her. Perhaps she was the blindest to it. Now, people all over the world were seeing her for the incredible person she was. More importantly, she was making a difference.

Jenn was more than just a public face for her followers. She was a cancer sister. Numerous women would reach out to her through Facebook and Twitter and share their stories. She always did her best to respond with care, sympathy, and thoughtfulness. In doing so, she made many friends. She would even make sure they had support groups on Facebook, and then she would make the extra effort to keep tabs on them.

She also did far more with her social media platforms than share her journey. Indeed, Jenn made great use of the time she was bed-bound, by following cancer research, as well as stories of people who had other terminal illnesses. Any time she found something interesting, whether it was positive or something she disagreed with – like Susan G. Komen for the Cure – she would share the link and her thoughts about it. When it came to awareness campaigns, she was adamantly against the "pink" image of cancer. "Cancer isn't pink," she said. To emphasize that point, she posted a very brave picture of her mangled chest with the words, "I am not a pink ribbon."

"No Bra Days do nothing to promote awareness," Jenn would say. Instead, what people need is education. She did everything she could to encourage people to check themselves regularly, and to promote little-known facts, such as how men and even animals can get breast cancer. Jenn fought to debunk common myths, like the idea that breast cancer is one of the better cancers to get, and educate people on how unique and adaptable each cancer is to the individual. She also promoted fundraisers for Metavivor.org, as well as money raising efforts for other patients who were either battling cancer, or who had recently died from it.

In return, her audience came to love and admire her. Eventually, she started to ask her followers to help our own family. The first time, she didn't have to, it just happened. Jenn had put her bucket list out there on the internet soon after she was diagnosed as terminal, and her followers responded in powerful ways. With their help and the assistance of some family members, we were able to carry out her bucket list, plus one item on mine. Because of the love, support and generosity of her online community, we got to make some genuinely incredible memories together. I will be forever grateful for that.

After Jenn died, I received countless messages of condolence and offers for support. There were so many sympathy notes, that I just found over a dozen more on my Facebook timeline while researching this book, which I had never encountered before, even though I did my best to keep up with them at the time. Many of these messages were by people hailing from all over the world, with stories about how they found Jenn and what a difference she had made in their life. An incredible, overwhelming tribute. What she had accomplished in the last part of her life is simply awe-inspiring.

In addition to the messages of condolence, other YouTubers she had bonded with along the way posted tribute videos. I've even seen her pop up in channels of people we never met, in videos along the lines of, "Top YouTubers Who Have Died and Will Be Missed." At least one musical performance at Angelo State University was dedicated in Jenn's memory, and this makes me wonder how many other dedications and tributes were done, that I'll never even know about.

This shows what a huge difference one seemingly ordinary individual can make in the world. We couldn't have possibly been prouder of her.

Not long after Jenn started documenting her journey, she began imploring me to do the same. I just couldn't. My stress and anxiety levels were escalating, and every spare moment of my time that I wasn't tending to her and the boys, I needed to escape into Minecraft and video editing. I didn't want to think about our situation any more than I already was, which was every moment I wasn't playing or editing. So, I chose not to share my side of the journey. At least for a long time.

In the Summer of 2016, we went to California on a trip sponsored by Ally's Wish, an organization which grants a last wish to young, terminally ill mothers with small children. One afternoon, while the boys and I were on a mid-day break, I was lying in bed next to Jenn. The kids were in the next room, separated by a set of not soundproofed double doors, playing on their electronics. I was watching an anime show on my laptop while Jenn was trying to take a nap. Then I saw it. She was quietly reaching her hand over to me. Something was wrong. I took her hand.

"My heart is freaking out," she said, "I'm scared to fall asleep. I feel like I could go at any moment." I shut my laptop, set it aside, took her hand and held her. I had been mentally preparing myself for the moment of her death. She always told me she wanted to die in my arms, and I needed to make sure I made that as comforting an experience as possible. I couldn't do that crying. So, I had spent several months, at least, playing out scenarios like this in my head, trying to get over the terror of it. The mental torture of that practice paid off. Now that the time had come, I was calm and collected.

I held her for a couple of minutes and told her everything was okay, and I would take care of the boys. "I don't want to die here," she said, "I want to die in my bed."

"I know."

"I don't want you to have to transport my body back to Texas, either. That's a pain in the ass," she continued.

"It's okay, babe. Don't worry about any of that. I'm here with you now. At least we weren't at the park. And if you die here, I'll take care of getting your body home. I'll take care of everything. You just relax and try not to worry about that stuff." I responded.

A couple of minutes had passed when I realized that, if this was it, then the boys should have a chance to say goodbye. At the same time, I didn't want to traumatize them unnecessarily if she lived. It wasn't often she said she felt like she was about to die, but it also wasn't the first time. I called the boys in.

"What's up, Dad?" Devin asked. "Is everything okay?"

"I just thought, your mom isn't feeling well, and she's about to try to take a nap, so I thought you guys should come in and give her a kiss and tell her you love her," I said, totally calm. Still, it was like they both knew what was going on. I could see it in their eyes, a look that said, *I guess this is it.* And I could be wrong about that because they were just as calm and collected as I was. They just seemed sad. They each took turns kissing her on the face and telling her they loved her, and then went back into their half of the suite.

Jenn later told me that she knew what I was doing. And she said to herself, Okay, Chris is here, I'm in his arms, the boys have said their goodbyes. I can go now. It's okay to go now, body. I don't want to die, but if it's time to go, then just go.

But it was not to be on that day. She fell asleep, perhaps thinking she was going to die, but didn't. I was relieved, but also sad and worried. Jenn was getting worse. Her pain was so severe, she couldn't go out with us for more than a few hours a day, and even that took an extreme effort on her end. She could only do it because she was entirely determined to make the most of her time with the boys. I knew she was in so much pain, and part of me wished it could have ended for her then. I didn't realize it at that moment, but it would have, in fact, been much better for all of us if it had.

After she woke up, we went to the parks, and bounced between California Adventures and the Magic Kingdom. It was a beautiful evening, and I am grateful we had that time together.

Later that night, back at the hotel room, I really needed to talk. Usually I vented to friends, but this time I took to Facebook. I told the story of what happened, and a breakdown I'd had the previous day over a status update, and received an overwhelming response. A couple of people asked if they could share it, which I was okay with, so I made that post public – my personal page's default is friends only.

There was a second incident later that month, while we were in San Antonio for a band director convention. I will provide more details later, but in short, something completely overwhelming happened, and I also went on Facebook to vent. Again, it was well received, with more requests to share. That was when I realized, not only was it helpful for me to write about what I was going through, but it could also help other people. Starting my own Facebook page made sense, because besides benefitting myself and others, if I continued to share my story after Jenn died, it would be a means of staying connected to her, and a great way to honor her legacy. That's how Coffee With Coop began.

Having this page was instrumental in my coping and healing process. Many of Jenn's followers came over, to hear my side of things, and to be able to keep up with our family after her death. They were and still are incredibly compassionate, kind, and supportive. Anytime I posted about parenting, work, or coping struggles, they were always there to cheer me on. It was nice to hear that many people say, "Hey, you're doing a great job, even if it doesn't feel like it." This community has been with me since I started documenting, reading my lengthy posts, and always supportive.

A few times people tried to be negative, which was quickly handled by the page admins, usually before I even knew what had happened. Aside from those few instances, Coffee With Coop's community has been an essential and somewhat unique part of my support network, and one for which I am forever grateful.

Sharing our journey on social media did a lot for our family. It was a place to vent, which is great, but it was also a way to help others. Cancer is such a senseless, terrible thing to happen to any family, and while it will never be worth the cost, letting others in on it can at least bring some meaning. It's fair to say we have received from our communities far more than we have given. Only with their help, after all, were we able to carry out Jenn's Bucket List and pay for most of her death expenses. The love and support helped us to keep our heads up under extreme duress. It also serves as a constant reminder that there are kind people all over the world, and restores one's faith in humanity. While it can get a little stressful, the benefits far outweigh the cost. It's been a fantastic, unique experience that has really helped both Jenn and myself.

Chapter 6

Piece By Piece

"There is a sacredness in tears. They are not the mark of weakness, but of power. They speak more eloquently than ten thousand tongues. They are the messengers of overwhelming grief, of deep contrition, and of unspeakable love."

– WASHINGTON IRVING

CANCER SUCKS. IT'S an epic emotional challenge and physical drain. Imagine climbing a mountain in freezing weather, and you can't see the peak. You've lost all sense of direction, and don't know how much further you have to go or how steep the path will get. There are blizzards and avalanches. Many times you want to give up. What awaits you at the peak is unknown. Will it be a clear view above the clouds, or just more ice fog? Quite possibly, you'll have to repeat the ascent more than once, each time with less resources.

Patient or caretaker, cancer changes you and your relationships forever, even if it ends in complete remission. While some of these changes might be for the better, the majority of them are for the worse.

First we lost our happiness. Jenn and I often explained to friends we were still happy as a married couple, but that it is simply impossible to be joyful when you're dealing with cancer. Who knows, perhaps that's not entirely true. Maybe there are people who can reach such a level of acceptance, they can brush aside their impending death or loss and fully enjoy life. Jenn and I couldn't. Instead we found ourselves in a constant state of anxiety, sadness and anger. The happiness we had worked so hard to achieve, vanished with the discovery of her cancer, and whatever joy remained was being chipped away over time.

Right after the diagnosis, Jenn wanted to go out and eat unhealthy food. Her mindset was, "This cancer is probably going to kill me anyway, I might as well enjoy what I eat!" Sadly, giving up her healthy habits became one of many regrets she would later have. It crossed my mind to say something, but I decided not to. I figured she was allowed, and it wasn't my place to judge. She never blamed me for overlooking her diet, but I still wonder if I did the right thing. Perhaps getting her to think about it from another perspective could have kept her in better shape, and with that, in higher spirits.

When Jenn got cancer, we had together lost over 160 pounds. We were very proud of our weight loss journeys, though they occurred at different times. Jenn had gotten heavier before starting treatment, but once she was on chemo and radiation, she had to take steroids, and those will cause weight gain regardless of one's diet. I can't remember how many pounds I put on, but at the end, Jenn was almost as large as she had ever been, and hated herself for that. She would look in the mirror, and between the lack of hair, mangled chest, and the fat that had returned, she felt like a monster.

I wish there was something more I could have done to help her. My reassurances that she was still beautiful, would always be beautiful to me, fell on deaf ears. I suppose there's a limit to how much a person can improve another one's self-image.

Chemotherapy and radiation did a lot more than cause weight gain. Chemo side effects vary wildly depending on the type you're taking. Some treatments cause your hair to fall out, others bring on bone and joint pain, or neuropathy. Some will weaken your gums, predisposing you to tooth loss. All of them make you tired. There are plenty of side effects I'm leaving out, but these are the main ones Jenn experienced. They all take a toll on your loved ones, as well as yourself. Dealing with those side effects was probably the most difficult aspect of the cancer battle.

Jenn before cancer and later in hospice.

The worst part is that the side effects accumulate over time. As the poison builds up in the body, both intensity and duration increase. Then again, the first treatment was also brutal. Jenn was in a tremendous amount of pain, and tried to sleep through as much of it as possible. But at least it lasted only for a relatively short period, and after that, she seemed fairly normal. The second chemotherapy was easier than the first, requiring two days of recovery at the most. I was feeling hopeful, this might not be as bad as we had feared. However, we both underestimated the accrual of adverse effects in addition to Jenn's ever-weakening state with each chemo infusion.

Eventually Jenn needed three days of recuperation, then we got to have her back for four. While she was recovering, she was mostly asleep, because when she wasn't, she was in agony from the bone pain and the tingling of the neuropathy.

"When is mom going to wake up, dad?" Kayden would ask.

"I don't know, buddy. But right now, mom needs her sleep, so she can start to feel better," I responded.

Our home was once a great place for the boys and their friends to hang out and play. We were the "cool house" on the block. As Jenn's treatments continued, she required more and more time to recover. Four days dealing with the after-effects, followed by three days of enjoying a somewhat normal life. Then it was five days of recovery. Jenn's need for a quiet place to rest necessitated new rules for the boys. Our house was no longer a place where kids could be kids.

It took a while for them to get used to having to be quiet all the time. Eventually, the boys adapted. No more yelling. No more running and acting crazy inside the house. The volume of the TV in the living room needed to be turned down low, as Jenn had always been a light sleeper. When Devin's friends came over, they were only allowed to hang out in his room, and if they got too loud, I had to send them home. I cannot imagine how this stunted the boys' ability to have fun and joy in their lives. But they're awesome kids, and once they understood it was important for mom to be able to sleep, they obliged and did not complain. Fortunately, children are very adaptable.

However, in addition to them having to give up their play space, Jenn was beginning to slip away. I was losing my wife, and the boys their mother. We trudged through the days of her being confined to the bedroom, eagerly awaiting the point at which she would be better.

Initially we thought it was rough when Jenn was bedridden for five or six days, and then had twenty-four hours of feeling okay. Later on though, she didn't fully recover at all before the next appointment. And things would only get worse.

The scans right after the completion of the initial cycle of chemotherapy provided us with a glimmer of hope. The tumor responded incredibly well to the first mixture of medications – Jenn was receiving two types of chemo at a time. It invigorated Jenn enough to keep putting herself through this hell.

But the cycle of deterioration continued. The next combination of drugs required treatment only once every other week. Great, we thought, she'll have a longer period of feeling well. Which was the case, at first. As time went on, however, the ratio of bad to good days shifted in favor of the bad. Ultimately, Jenn would be recovering for a week and a half, followed by maybe three or four decent days. Throughout her last chemotherapy, which at that point was strictly for pain control, there were no more good days, only ones with less agony than she would have been in without treatment. Considering the pain chemo caused all on its own, that is saying something.

As mentioned earlier, during radiation therapy Jenn was gone for extended periods of time. It sadly gave us an eerie preview of life without her. Maybe that was a blessing in disguise, making it easier to transition into being without Jenn eventually. It was stressful, particularly when I had to bring the boys along with me to after school work duties. But I think it also toughened us up.

You might think something as traumatic as cancer would bring you and your spouse closer together, but that wasn't the case for us. We were still close, we loved each other until the end, but our ability to communicate diminished more and more as time went on.

It started with not being able to cry together. Perhaps we should have made it a thing between us, that it would be okay and normal to shed tears in each other's presence. It did happen a few times, and then we felt more connected. It was as if we had found each other again. Every time we agreed that it should be okay and occur more often. I don't know why it didn't. I suppose the instinct of wanting to be strong for the other person was too powerful to allow for it.

Eventually, we didn't talk much about our emotions at all, at least not as often as we should have been.

We didn't want to burden each other. Jenn knew I wanted her to be happy, and she also knew that seeing her deteriorate both physically and emotionally was damaging my mental health. I'm guessing she didn't open up to her mom very often, either, for the same reason. So she chose to vent to her friends instead, especially the cancer sisters she met through Facebook, as well as her best friends. If it was late, overwhelming, or impossible to hide, she came to me. And when she did, I was there to comfort her.

The same way Jenn understood how her state was affecting me, I knew, through the conversations we did have, that the pain the boys and I were experiencing caused her intense guilt. She felt so guilty indeed, she often questioned whether to keep fighting, or just stop treatment so she would depart sooner, and allow us to start healing. After she was given the terminal diagnosis, this was constantly on her mind. As much as I wanted to open up and talk to Jenn about my thoughts and feelings, I was worried it might only add to the weight of that guilt on her heart. Perhaps not venting enough to her or the people around me was another reason I was so enthralled with Minecraft.

We lost the open communication we'd had for almost our entire marriage. We could cry with each other, but we tried not to. We didn't talk as much as we used to, because of the potential pain and guilt inflicted on the other person. We never completely drifted apart, but the closeness we shared when we were open and wholly in love with each other, was gone.

I'm only mentioning this next point in the interest of full disclosure and honesty. It should come as no surprise that between our lack of communication, Jenn being insecure about her body and generally feeling unwell, our sex life suffered. Initially it diminished, until eventually, it was non-existent. What's worse, the last few attempts we made, spread out over several weeks to months, were painful for her. Jenn's body simply didn't work the way it used to.

Of course I completely understood, but that didn't make it less frustrating. Sex is listed as one of the basic human needs. Understanding doesn't eliminate that need. Still, I was careful to never force the issue, or make Jenn feel guilty about not being well enough for sex. After all, it simply wasn't her fault. Instead, I accepted it as part of cancer life, and tried to cope as best I could.

I've heard horror stories of men cheating on their cancer-stricken wives because of this dilemma. All I can say is, please, don't be that person. Being sexually frustrated is difficult, I get it. But you have to remember how much your spouse loves you, and what it means to them that you're walking by their side through these dire times. If you hang in there, and take care of them, you are a true hero.

Keep in mind, it's simply not their fault. Your spouse didn't ask for this, and there's a good chance they already feel inadequate not having as much sex as they used to, or not being able to at all. Jenn told me she carried a lot of guilt about this. In fact, once she was unable to have sex, one of her biggest regrets was that we didn't have more of it when she was healthy. She had let her insecurities get in the way of enjoying sex. These were self-doubts about her weight, or related to how previous men had treated her. I did everything I could to make her feel safe and not judged, but those insecurities were deeply ingrained. Despite being very much in love, our sex life was never as active as other couples claim theirs is, so I was used to experiencing that frustration occasionally, though it got worse with cancer. It was Jenn's biggest regret about our marriage in general. In her videos she stressed the importance of enjoying your health while you have it, and that is part of what she meant. If your spouse's sex drive has decreased due to treatment, you have to accept that and not blame them. It doesn't make it any less frustrating, but there are other ways to deal with it besides infidelity.

Finally, I would like to remind you of the promise you made when you got married. Jenn and I went through all of our vows. Cancer is the "...through sickness," and, "for worse," part of it. Depending on your beliefs, you may have even made this commitment in front of your creator. When you choose the one you marry, they become the single most important person in your world. We prioritized each other over our children – which is the bible's advice, and good advice, I think. You chose them to be the most important person in your life, "...until death do you part." This is the hard part, but you can do this. The whole cancer business is tough, and this only adds to the stress. But don't let sex be the straw that broke the marriage's back. Most reprehensible are the stories of guys leaving their wives for other women, who are also leaving children behind. There is absolutely no way a cancer patient is going to be able to properly provide for their kids all by themselves. These poor excuses for men not only abandon their wives when they need them the most, but their children, too.

Don't be like them. You are better than that. It is tough, but you can see this through. You don't have to be perfect; just hang in there and do what you can. You've got this.

I missed Jenn's old personality. I am not saying this to vilify her, but she changed a lot, in some ways for the better, but in many ways for the worst.

She didn't change completely. For example, she never lost her love of pranks, or her sense of humor, although it did turn much darker over time. At least when she was joking about death, she was still joking. I didn't mind the dark humor. It gave her a chance to vent, and a way to laugh in the face of death.

Jenn never stopped loving us with all her might. As time went on, she wasn't always able to express it, but we never doubted her love. She rarely requested to be alone while she was awake, although we did allow for that. Instead, she tried to be in the living room, and when she couldn't do that, she encouraged us to hang out in the bedroom with her. We had a lot of great talks lying in bed. It was where she planted the seed in my brain that I would be happy again someday.

But there were other changes. How could there not be? Jenn went from enjoying a dream life to receiving a death sentence against her will, without having done anything wrong. Who wouldn't be angry, bitter, stressed, depressed, anxious, et cetera? These emotions manifested themselves in swearing, outbursts, having less patience, and so forth. Just as I had to be gentle with myself, I had to be gentle with Jenn. She refused to go to therapy with me, so I needed to accept that she was coping the best she could.

On the positive side, she became more outspoken. It seems common among people with terminal cancer to stop caring about what everyone thinks of them, and start voicing their honest opinions. This allowed Jenn to be open about her journey when posting on YouTube or social media platforms, as well as expose Susan G. Komen for the Cure for their sketchy practices, while at the same time promoting Metavivor and

Death With Dignity. It gave her the courage to become the rock star I always knew she was.

A difficult issue I had to confront was the sense of having lost my future. It was one thing to cope with the fact that the incredible life Jenn and I had built together was gone forever, but it was another thing entirely, to consider a future without her.

Jenn was my best friend and soulmate, we loved each other immensely, and had so much fun. We had every intention of spending the rest of our lives together, raising our children, and ribbing each other as an elderly couple. She was going to support me as I climbed the career ladder, and after retirement we had planned on traveling the world, and enjoying life in ways we weren't able to yet. We didn't have all the details figured out, but we were happy, and very much looking forward to our future together.

Everything we had worked for seemed to have lost its purpose, now that Jenn was not going to be there. I was afraid of having to start over, especially since I had the boys to care for. Truthfully, I thought the challenge would be too great.

I worried about feeling lonely, depressed and angry for the rest of my life. In this dystopian scenario of mine, the depression would not allow me to hang onto my job as a band director, having lost all passion for music anyway. Because I would lack energy and a love for life, I'd go home and have no strength or enthusiasm for my children. I'd probably be neglectful, wanting to be by myself all of the time – although I still knew I'd at least provide what they required in terms of basic needs, and make sure they were taking care of themselves. Then, as a result of my bad parenting, I figured the chances were high my boys would end up as drug addicts, bitter, angry jerks, possibly criminals of some sort. Even though I knew they were amazing kids, I just didn't see how they could possibly emerge from this situation as good people, especially with a terrible dad like I was going to be. There were countless times I wished I had gotten cancer instead of Jenn, thinking that if the boys could only have one of us around to parent them, Jenn would do a much better job. Finally, because I would be too depressed and not interested in finding new love, I'd probably resort to sex hookup websites or just straight up prostitutes. None of this I would even consider under normal circumstances, but it was the nightmare I pictured my future to be.

Then something amazing happened. When I shared this vision of my fate with Jenn, she hated it. We were lying in bed, and she asked me about my future without her, so I outlined my dire prediction. Jenn did not want that for the boys or me. She convinced me I could be happy again someday, that it would get better with time. She said she didn't like me being alone for too long, that I should find a new love as soon as I was ready for it. Granted, she was incredibly jealous that someone else would get to be with me the way she had been. Jenn hated it, resenting the fact that it couldn't be her any longer. But more than anything, she wanted me to be happy, and that weighed heavier than her ego. Jenn never gave me a timeframe for when I could start dating. Instead, she kept reiterating that I should move on with my life, try to be happy, and also help the boys find happiness again.

Talking about this subject matter always felt awkward. It was impossible to imagine myself with anyone else, so discussing that on top of my uncertain future was uncomfortable for me. I am glad we did have the conversations though. Jenn was trying to prepare me for life without her, and it turns out she made a big impact. Whenever I felt any guilt about moving on, her words echoed through my head, and I knew that not only was it okay, it was what she wanted. Pushing forward meant honoring her wishes for myself and the boys.

Jenn wasn't just getting me ready, she was simultaneously preparing the kids, her best friends, and her mother. With her mom, Jenn stressed the importance of being there for the boys, how she had to keep living for them, and that I would also need her support. She even talked to her about my dating again after her death, and how she wanted that for me.

Jenn helped me create a different vision of my future. It took a lot of work on her end, but I figured it out eventually, months before she died. This gave me the time to prepare for what was to come, and be optimistic about it. It made the transition to life without her so much easier.

Many times, when Jenn tried to ease my mind about the future, I refused to believe her. My lost passion for music and teaching for instance. Jenn had staunchly supported me while I was studying to become a band director, and without her in my life, it seemed pointless. Though I continued to try my best, work simply didn't matter anymore. Nothing did besides my family. Lying in bed, lamenting to Jenn about the issue, she said reassuringly, "Don't worry, babe. It will come back. After I'm gone."

"I sure hope you're right about that." I responded.

And she was. She was absolutely right. About everything.

Being a single parent is tough. You hear that all the time, but it really is stressful. Rewarding, but taxing. I was slowly losing my co-parent.

The more you think about it, the more emotional it gets, because your spouse, if it is the biological parent, is the person you made these babies with. We have an amazing picture of Jenn holding Devin as a newborn. I wish we had a similar photo with Kayden, but I can't find one. At the time I was teaching myself Adobe Photoshop, so I did a bit of editing, added names to the image, printed and framed it. Whenever I look at that picture, all the memories of the different experiences we had during each pregnancy come flooding back. How Devin was a surprise, but Kayden took several months to conceive, which added its own drama and heartache. How Jenn's personality, while pregnant, reflected each of the boys' personalities as newborns. Then of course the actual births, the emotions and excitement from those days, and what the boys were like as infants and throughout their first year.

We went through so much together, shared countless happy and sad moments, an entire history. It's heartbreaking when you lose your partner and co-parent, and with Jenn's slow decline, I saw it happening a little bit at a time.

It's also physically draining, because you have to take on more of the responsibilities around the house. As the cancer progressed, Jenn started cooking less, doing less laundry and cleaning. I had a tough time adjusting, and was not picking up the slack for a long time, mostly because I was depressed and lacked the motivation.

While Jenn was still well enough to be in the living room, she could at least help discipline the boys, hang out with us, be present. Slowly, that went away, too, until either the chemotherapy side effects or the cancer pain kept her in bed all the time.

It was extremely important to Jenn to participate in the boys' lives as much as possible. Even when she was practically bed bound, she called them in to ask about their days, and carry out special little rituals. For instance, she regularly had the boys put their hands and feet up to each others to compare sizes, let them see how much they had grown, and how close they were to being as large as her hands and feet. She used these intimate moments to counsel them, and provide sage advice I only wish I had the wisdom to give. Then there were her special hugs. Devin commented on missing them one night after she was gone, as I was hugging him goodnight.

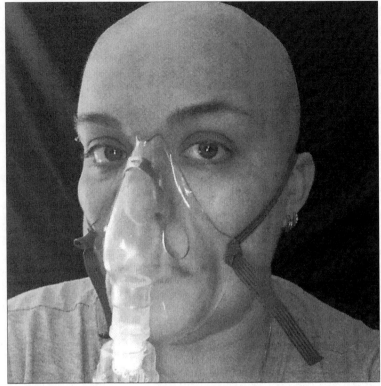

One of Jenn's last selfies during hospice.

After I had been in therapy and on medication for a few months, Jenn got to see my improved efforts around the house. I started completing the nighttime routine on my own more often. Jenn still helped with brushing teeth or reading to the boys, but I did most of it. Next came laundry, though I was hardly on top of that.

I was also receiving additional support. Jenn's mom helped as much as she could when she was around, and a dear friend paid for a housekeeping service to straighten up for us once a week. This was a huge relief, since cleaning was my least favorite chore.

While Jenn and I were on our second honeymoon as part of our bucket list, I started to cook. I felt quite apprehensive about it. The last time I had prepared a hot meal was when we were living in the apartment in San Angelo, I was still in college and we were both obese. The dishes I knew how to make were limited to Hamburger Helper, extremely unhealthy tortillas, and artery-clogging wrapped bratwurst. I had no idea how to cook anything, much less anything healthy. Before we left on our trip, Jenn had sent me a link on YouTube, to go from "Noob to Pro" in the kitchen. It was a humorous video with simple, yet practical cooking tips. It showed an easy way to sear steaks, so during our honeymoon I cooked my first steak since ruining one in college. It tasted pretty mediocre, but Jenn encouraged me, and so I kept on going.

My goal was to learn how to prepare five healthy and tasty dinners. I personally don't mind eating the same meals repeatedly, and I figured my kids wouldn't have a choice.

I started posting pictures – often called "food porn" – of my early creations on Facebook. Seeing them now, I think they look awful, especially the sides, prepared from frozen bags. But everyone was cheering me on, including Jenn, who continued to share her tips with me, most of which I promptly rejected. It took her over an hour to fix a meal, and that was too long for me. My goal was to make dinner in thirty minutes to an hour. While Jenn cooked everything at lower temperatures, I wanted to figure out how to do it at medium to medium hot. After burning a bunch of meals, I learned to mostly restrain myself to medium on the stove.

My cooking skills have improved since then. I even get compliments from the boys, and occasionally from visitors such as my dad or Jenn's mom. I still don't enjoy the process, but listening to music or podcasts helps, and I'm glad people are happy to eat my food.

It is important to me to serve healthy meals in our house. Early on I was bringing home a lot of fast food, which was the reason we were all gaining weight. Even though I felt terrible doing that to my family, I continued, because I was depressed and lacked the motivation to cook. Everything is infinitely harder when you're trapped in depression.

Over time, as I started to feel better, I had more energy to complete household tasks. I did the laundry, cooking, cleaning, yard work, and anything else that came up, on top of helping the boys with their school work, and mostly running the nighttime routine on my own. I toughened up and adapted. At least I got to transition into being a single parent gradually.

It must be worse for people who lose their co-parent suddenly, because they don't have the luxury of a slow changeover. It takes a while to grow strong enough to be able to do everything for your children, and in the meantime, whom do the kids have? That is a tough situation, and if that happens to be you, I am so very sorry.

The only upside – if you can call it that – to losing your loved one slowly over time, as opposed to suddenly, is that it allows you to grieve every little piece individually, rather than all at once. I do not know which is easier. Everyone's grieving process is difficult, regardless of the circumstances, and who are we to say whose is worse? I consider myself lucky because it happened gradually, but I didn't exactly have a choice in the matter. Part of me feels bad for saying that, because there were many times when, for Jenn's sake, I wish it had been much faster. But I can't deny that it helped to be able to slowly work my way into this new life rather than being thrust into it all at once. Besides, the extra time with Jenn was precious to us.

I had a memorable conversation with the dad of a student. He's the leader of a youth group at a local church, an incredible guy, and I always enjoy talking to him and, on occasion, his wife. One day, I learned they had lost their two-year-old daughter to an illness. It sounded harrowing. This wasn't their first child, but she was born with congenital disabilities and struggled just to live. They decided to keep the baby, and give her the best possible life they could. It wasn't easy, but her condition improved, and for a while, it looked like she was going to beat the odds. Then, after a couple of years, her health sharply declined, and seemingly in the blink of an eye, she was gone.

His story broke my heart. We stood in the school cafeteria as he recalled the events, and I said to him, "I think you have it way harder than I do. I can't imagine losing a child."

"No, man. I think you have it harder. I can't imagine losing your wife over time like that. It had to be gut-wrenching to watch her slowly fade away."

We quickly realized how pointless it was to compare tragedies. The truth is, they both sucked, probably equally, but in different ways.

Once I started looking for silver linings, I found comfort in having been able to grieve each piece of Jenn as it went. It allowed a much gentler transition for myself and the boys.

Chapter 7

Mom is Dying

"Motherhood: All love begins and ends there."

– ROBERT BROWNING

PEOPLE ALWAYS SAY how resilient children are, and it's true. Kids adapt far quicker than adults, but that doesn't mean they don't need help. I knew the boys were losing a big piece of their world, just like I was, but it was easy for me to get so caught up in my grief, that I didn't give the boys the attention they needed. So, I guarded against that by constantly trying to see the situation through their eyes.

Early on in treatment, Jenn slept a lot to recover from the side effects of chemotherapy. If she felt well enough, she moved to the couch to spend the evening with us, and do her part of the nighttime routine. More fundamentally, at the time of Jenn's diagnosis, she had been a very active person and loved playing with the boys, engaging in tickle fights, even roughhousing. She incorporated them into her workouts, had them exercise next to her, or used them as weights. They loved every minute.

As the chemotherapy set in, Jenn didn't have the energy or strength to do that anymore. While she was recovering after each treatment, the boys were missing out. It wasn't so bad at first, but as the situation became continuous, and Jenn's recuperation periods lengthened, they felt that loss deeply. Engaging in physical play with mom was not possible anymore.

Jenn did her best to remain a presence in the boys' lives. She was adamant that if she couldn't be there for the boys, then what was the point of continuing treatment? So, whenever she had the strength to be with us, she was, even if it meant her pain got worse. Eventually, due to the lesions on her diaphragm, it became unbearable for her to sit at all.

Life at home had to become increasingly quiet. As mentioned before, our house used to be the one Devin's friends wanted to hang out at. It was probably because of the video games, but I like to think our loving, positive atmosphere had something to do with it, too. Whatever the reasons were, they slowly faded away.

The boys had to learn to accommodate Jenn's need for rest, which meant avoiding loud noises at all costs. They understood, but the fun factor was gone, our house now a sad and silent place to be.

Another difficult change for the boys and myself was the way Jenn's personality changed as her condition worsened. Jenn had been a true role model mother before cancer. She was happy, in great shape, took excellent care of us, made sure to always let us know how much we were loved, had an open line of communication with the boys, I could go on and on. I want to focus on the role model part in the subsequent paragraphs.

Jenn reached a certain point I've heard referred to as, "Beyond the fuck it." Her bitterness toward the lousy hand life had unfairly dealt her became increasingly difficult to mask, even around the boys. She gradually lost her patience with them. Parenting is challenging enough, but doing it while you're in constant pain from cancer, chemo, radiation, or all of the above, has got to be exponentially harder. I don't think anyone could be graceful about it one hundred percent of the time.

Swearing was Jenn's main outlet for her frustration. We had always kept our cursing away from the kids, and avoided vulgar music and media around them. But at some point Jenn stopped caring. She began allowing herself to swear in the presence of the children. On long road trips she wanted to listen to her music, and I wasn't going to say no. Her life was too short for that.

Again, I'm not sharing this to vilify Jenn, but it was bothering the boys and myself. I approached her about the issue once, and she explained it to me like this, "Chris, I only have so much patience, okay? I have a limited amount of patience. This cancer is all over my body. All of the pain that causes, the treatments, the chemo side effects, all of that shit takes up all of my patience! So, I just don't have any left. I'm really sorry, but I'm doing the best I can!" For me, that was all it took to let it go.

After I understood where she was coming from and what she was going through, I needed to explain it to Devin and Kayden. When they pulled me into our safe zone, they wanted to know why mom was meaner than she used to be. I clarified that she was hurting badly, but still loved them as much as she always had. Then I asked if they could try to be patient with her, and reassured them that it wasn't their fault, that mom would never talk to them this way if it weren't for the pain.

Jenn had come up with the idea of creating a safe space in the house, called "The Bubble," which we are still using today. Inside, the boys can say anything, including swear words, as long as they're not disrespectful toward the adults. If there is ever anything they feel uncomfortable approaching us about, they can ask us to join them in the bubble. Eventually they stopped using a specific area, and now the entire house is the bubble. It was a good place for us to have the more difficult conversations back then, and it remains helpful to this day.

These issues are upsetting enough to adults, but they have to be immensely hurtful for children.

How we spoke to the boys, who were only seven and three years old, was crucial in helping them comprehend and cope with what was happening. When the time came, we had to convey the fact that mom was going to die, and we, but mostly Jenn, tried to prepare them as much as possible. I had done a lot of reading on the subject before our first conversation about cancer. All the experts agree it's best to be honest with your children rather than attempt to hide it, which is almost impossible anyway. So, that's exactly what we did. Though we still had to translate everything into kid language, without going into too much detail about what Jenn was having to endure.

This was more difficult than it sounds. I wish I were as good at talking to Devin and Kayden as Jenn was. She had an amazing knack for getting on their level, using age appropriate terms to help them understand complicated ideas. She really was a wonderful mother.

We explained to the boys that mommy is sick, and with the kind of illness that lasts a very long time. We gave them the same timeline we were working with, which was about one year of treatment, surgery, and recovery. Any questions they had, we tried to answer as openly as we could, explaining how Jenn's medicine would make her very tired, and sometimes even cause pain. We told them it might also change her appearance, and that her hair would fall out.

But we always reassured them it was okay. Mommy didn't mind if she lost her hair. We kept it upbeat. Jenn's mom had fought breast cancer more than twelve years ago, so we used her as a positive precedent. "Memaw had breast cancer, too, and she's back to normal now!" Admittedly, Cindy is far from being back to normal. Her cancer treatment left her with lymphoma, and other permanent side effects, as it would for Jenn, but they didn't need to know these details. Cindy had been that way for the boys since they were born, so it made sense to them.

We never intended on telling them that cancer could be fatal. At least not before Jenn's status became terminal. Regrettably, that decision was taken from us, when Jenn brought them to a friend's house one day. They were playing with her friend's boys, while the daughters, who were a bit older, stayed in the kitchen with the moms. At some point the conversation turned to Jenn explaining to her friend how we talked to the kids about the cancer, and that we had omitted any possibility of a fatal outcome. One of the daughters was surprised by this and, quite loudly, asked, "You haven't told them it could kill you?"

Sadly, just at that moment, Devin happened to be running down the hallway and overheard. His little heart probably broke, and it is difficult for me to imagine the emotional mix of confusion, disbelief, and ultimate betrayal he must have felt. He walked into the kitchen with big, teary eyes and said, "Mom, could your cancer really kill you?"

If only I had been there to assist in the situation and console him. However, the subject did come up again later on the same day, and then I was part of the effort to reassure the boys. To keep it positive, we focused on telling them survivor stories. As far as we were concerned, Jenn was going to beat this thing, and that's what we wanted our kids to know and believe in.

The real controversy started after Jenn had received her terminal diagnosis. Do we tell the boys their mom was going to die, or not. Our family members had conflicting opinions, so I did some research. As before, all the literature I found said to be upfront with children, and we followed that advice. We did exclude the gruesome details of what she may have to go through, and instead focused on the remaining time we would have together. Nobody had given us an idea of how long that period might be, but we did assure the boys that mommy was going to do everything the doctors told her to, so she could stay for as long as possible. Mom wasn't dying soon, in fact, she could be alive for years.

As Jenn got worse, Kayden often asked at bedtime, "Dad, what if mom dies tonight?" He was afraid of going to sleep, and her being dead the next morning. His eyes teared up, his lip pouty. It broke my heart every single time.

My answers were along the lines of, "Well, buddy, I can promise mom isn't going to die tonight. She'll be with us for a very long time." If he pressed the issue, I'd respond with something like, "It's true that she's going to die from the cancer. But it takes a long time, so she's going to be alive for a very long time. So, try not to worry about it. Mom will be around for a long time." I could say that honestly, because, to a four-year-old, even a couple of months feel like an eternity. When Devin asked that question, I responded the same way.

I tried to reassure the boys that everything was okay, and that it would continue to be okay. Dad would take excellent care of them and mom. Jenn's role was to help them understand what was happening to her, and ultimately prepare them for life without her.

She figured out a way to explain to both brothers, by then four and eight years old, what cancer is, why it spread, and how her body tried to fight it, but that the cancer was too strong. Jenn even talked about life without her. She went so far as to tell these boys I might marry another woman one day, and what that could be like, and how to handle it. Writing about this makes me tear up.

The strength it must have taken her, to keep it together while explaining to her sons how and why she was dying, and how to live life without her, is unimaginable. But she did it, and she did it well. Our boys were sad about losing their mom, but they understood what was happening to her, and they started contemplating being without her. The second part is huge, because that was my major breakthrough in recovery. I doubt anyone could have done a better job of preparing them for life without mom.

Although once I did explain an abstract concept to Devin in a way he understood. He had come up to me, starting to talk about his mom. I can't remember the details of the conversation, but he said with a dull look in his eyes, "Dad, I can't feel the light anymore. All I feel is darkness."

I was stunned. What could I say? I replied, "I'm sorry, Devin. I know it feels like everything is dark right now, but it won't stay dark forever. One day things will start to get better, and you'll find that light again. It's just going to take some time."

"How will I know? I can't even remember what the light feels like."

I realized the light was happiness. More than that, the light was love. Instinctively, I brought him in for a hug, but unbeknownst to him, I had set a trap....for tickling. I unleashed my tickle attack, catching him completely off guard. He started giggling, and I continued for a minute or so. Then I wanted to truly hug him. He was skeptical, but I reassured him until he caved, and let me envelope him in my arms. "Do you feel a little better now?"

"Yeah," he said.

"Do you feel that good feeling in your chest?" I said.

"Yeah, I think so."

"That's the light, Devin. It hasn't gone away completely. It's always there, and it will always be there, no matter how dark things get. Even if you can't feel it for a long time, it's still there. And one day, things will get better for us, and the light will come back, and you'll feel it all the time. I promise, one day, we'll be happy again."

Devin got it. He was still a bit unsure, but the message was received. It was the first time I felt as adept as Jenn at translating an abstract concept into little kid terms. Somehow, I had conveyed to a nine-year-old that the light he was describing represented love and happiness, and that while he thought it was gone, it really wasn't. I had also committed myself to more tickle fights with the boys.

We picked up several children's books to read to Kayden, to augment our explanations. Devin was a bit too old for them, but we shared them with him anyway. There was Mom Has Cancer by Jennifer Moore-Malinos. It's written from a child's perspective, and begins with a boy noticing that his parents are acting strange, and he can't figure out why. They tell him his mom has cancer, and what that will entail. Then it goes through how life changes during treatment, and ends on the upbeat note that his mom's cancer went away, and everything goes back to normal.

Another one we read was The Cancer That Wouldn't Go Away: A story for kids about metastatic cancer by Hadassa Field. It follows a boy named Max, and is very detailed for a children's book. He says how confusing it is that his mom has hair, but she's still sick. It illustrates the awkwardness and frustration kids encounter when they try to explain mom's condition to other children, and the inherent impatience they feel while waiting to find out whether or not a treatment is working. His mother keeps telling him, "One day at a time." Max has to handle not knowing what will happen, which I think is a core issue. Adults struggle with the concept of an uncertain future, so it must be that much harder for children. The book continually reinforces the theme of, "One day at a time." Jenn's version of that was, "This too, shall pass." The story touches a little bit on mom's ultimate decline, but it doesn't venture too far into that, nor does it mention her dying.

Both these books are sad, but they gently introduce young kids to cancer, how the disease may impact their lives, and what to expect going forward. Kayden and Devin were encouraged to follow certain routines – such as helping to take care of mommy and let her rest. It also pushed them to be more patient.

The third book we selected, and easily the most gut-wrenching yet helpful one, was Badger's Parting Gifts by Susan Varley. We read it when Jenn was close to death, and a few times after she had died. The story follows a group of small animals, but is told mostly from the perspective of Badger, an elderly, but dependable friend who is close to death. He isn't sick, just old. We hear how much he misses the times when he could still move around and run in the fields, and how that makes him not afraid of dying. Instead, he is worried about his friends after he will be gone. One night he sits in his rocking chair by the fire and falls asleep, dreaming that he's walking down a tunnel. It is a good dream, because his body feels light. He discards his cane and begins to run like he could when he was younger. This transition into death is portrayed as a freeing experience, rather than a sad one. The rest of the book describes his friends discovering Badger has died, and how they reflect on their fondest moments with him. These memories and everything they learned from Badger become his parting gifts, which will stay with them forever. I felt it was particularly important for Kayden. As difficult as it was for me to read and for him to hear, the uplifting depiction of death reinforced what we had previously told him; mainly that it wasn't going to be painful for mom, and how afterwards, she would be free from all the hurt and misery. There was also comfort in the idea that she would be with us forever, in our memories and through everything she taught us.

There are numerous books like these available, and in my experience it's a great way to help children comprehend difficult subject matters. They easily open up deep conversations, which need to happen if a family is affected by cancer.

At one point in our journey I received a call from the school. Both Devin's and Kayden's teachers wanted to talk to us about worrisome behaviors they had exhibited in class.

Adrian agreed to cover for me, so I could attend the meeting with Jenn. Most of the ones I held had been in classrooms, or via phone and e-mail. This was different. We went into the school's conference room, which had a long table surrounded by nice chairs, though there was little space to walk around. Both Jenn and I were a little intimidated by the atmosphere, as well as being in this place with Devin's and Kayden's entire educational teams, including the principal, during the school day. It meant all these teachers were missing class to be there, which I know requires a lot of organization and resources. This was obviously a big deal.

We had met everyone at the beginning of the school year at the Meet the Teacher night, but reintroduced ourselves anyway and shook hands. Then we got to it.

Devin's emotions manifested through anger, and he had been lashing out at classmates. So far he hadn't done anything physical, thankfully, but his teachers were worried it might escalate to that. The anger showed up in his drawings as well. A recent picture showed a scarecrow covered in blood, with an arrow and a machete through its head, and a dead person nearby, also covered in blood. Devin had never drawn images like that until Jenn became terminal.

Kayden suffered from general depression. One day in class they were doing a "Sharing Circle", where every kid can share their feelings. How great is that? In my opinion, people of all ages should get to have a sharing circle. What a wonderful teacher he had, and what a clever way to teach children to express themselves.

When it was Kayden's turn to speak, he said, "Sometimes I want to kill myself." Imagining these words coming from my little boy about broke my heart. His teacher recounted she immediately pulled him into her arms, told him how sad she would be if that happened, and how much she loved him.

The entire class chimed in, "We love you too, Kayden!" She said after hearing how loved he was, he calmed down and felt better, but obviously the incident concerned her. She had so far never encountered any major problems with Kayden, and we were shocked and surprised to hear her story. He did mention death every now and then, but never in the context of him dying.

The principal spoke. "We're doing our best to help the boys cope. Once a week we pull them out to visit with the counselor, so they have someone to talk to, but she isn't trained for a situation like this. We've been trying very hard to support your boys through this, and I know you're doing everything you possibly can. Nonetheless, we're obviously concerned, and they seem to be getting worse. We would really like for you to find the boys some professional counseling. I am convinced it is critical that you do so."

I felt incredibly stupid and neglectful. Of *course* they needed professional counseling. I was seeing a therapist, and had tried to convince Jenn to go with me. Why *wouldn't* the boys need therapy, too? I couldn't believe I had let my own grief cloud my judgment. I was naturally agreeing with the principal's recommendation, but had to ask one important question.

"I've been seeing a therapist for about six months now, but the office is in Odessa. Getting there in time for an appointment means I have to go during the day. I'm sure it will be the same for the boys, so they'll be missing a lot of school. My therapy schedule is once every other week, and it would probably be easiest if they went with me on those same days. Do you think they'll be able to stay caught up?" I wasn't so much asking if they could do it, but rather letting them know my kids would have to miss quite a bit of school – being absent more than ten percent of the time normally has major consequences – and was that okay with them?

The principal responded. "Chris, your kids are very bright. I don't have any concerns they wouldn't be able to stay caught up. We really want you to do whatever you have to, to get them the support they need." The other teachers agreed with this sentiment, so I promised to find a solution as soon as possible.

Unbelievably, getting them started on therapy took months. We had to wait at least thirty days before I could have a consultation, which merely meant that an assistant and I were going over the details of the boys' case. The first appointment for a session of their own was yet another month later. The practice had their reasons. Apparently most people don't show up to the consultation, so they won't schedule any further dates until afterward. This particular therapist was typically booked up at least four weeks in advance. Still, my one complaint about the office is that it should not take two months to get children their much needed help.

My therapy days turned into Cooper Family Therapy Days. We drove to Odessa in the morning, then one of the brothers got to have their forty-five minute session, while the other stayed with me in the lobby. To pass the time, we messed around on our electronic devices. My mom regularly met us for lunch, then she took Devin and Kayden to the mall while I went to my appointment with Misty in the afternoon.

The boys were given a lot of options when it came to their therapy. They got to choose between several areas, among them a doll room, play room, art room, plus a few others. As they were talking to the therapist, they could engage in board games, play with toys, or create art. They were looking forward to the appointments. Devin preferred tabletop games in the art space, while Kayden favored the art and play rooms for their plethora of toys and costumes.

Devin, Kayden and I waiting for their appointments.

Talking to their therapist affirmed my deep guilt about not getting them into counseling sooner. She explained, "If you think about it, the boys are dealing with everything you are, but they don't possess the coping skills you do." I knew she wasn't scolding me, but I beat myself up over it pretty hard.

She was a wonderful therapist, teaching the boys various ways to express their emotions, rather than holding them in, reinforcing that how they felt was normal under the circumstances. We had told them that last part many times, but I think hearing it from an outsider made a big difference. Throughout the summer, both Devin's and Kayden's mental health vastly improved, as they articulated their feelings and put any extra energy into healthy, positive outlets.

I had read that children who are losing a parent, often revert to an earlier stage of development. In our case the boys were more prone to throwing fits or acting selfishly, in addition to showing typical symptoms associated with depression, such as a lack of energy and motivation, random outbursts, anger issues, and others I've probably forgotten. I had to remember to be as gentle with the boys as I had learned to be with myself, when they weren't behaving up to our normal standards.

It was a difficult balancing act. While you have to accept a certain amount of acting out, you don't want them to be completely unhinged. Jenn was always telling them, "You can't use my having cancer as a reason to be bad," or "After I'm gone, you can't use my death as an excuse to be a bad person."

I can't emphasize enough how challenging it was, and the longer the situation went on, the less confident I became in my parenting. Was I being too hard, too soft? I was certainly more lenient than I used to be, but was that still too strict? In the end I had to follow my instincts.

We were very lucky to enroll both our kids into the extraordinary Camp Kesem. It is free, exclusively for children impacted by cancer. They all have a parent who either had it, is currently in treatment, or has died from it. This was huge for Devin and Kayden. Nobody at their school had been able to relate to what they were going through. Every single person at this camp got it. Most of the counselors were former campers, so they knew exactly what the kids were dealing with, too.

I'm not sure how we found out about it. I think the credit belongs to one of Jenn's social media followers. The first summer, Kayden was too young by one year, but Devin had been put on a waiting list. When we heard he actually got in, we were so excited for him.

We drove six hours to the camp, which is located just outside Austin. This one is hosted by the University of Texas – Austin Chapter of Camp Kesem, but it's a national organization. Devin was nervous and a bit afraid when we got there. First we had to stand in line for some time. The other kids were asking him what his camp name was, and he had no clue what to pick. We had discussed ideas on the way, but while in line I suggested Link, after the hero of the Legend of Zelda game franchise – which both boys love, but especially Devin, who has all kinds of Link and Zelda merchandise. He decided to go with that.

Everybody gathered in a room to wait until all of the attendees were processed. The counselors and campers had created a tunnel at the door. When someone new walked in, they cheered, hooted and hollered, gave high fives, and generally made a huge scene. Devin wasn't having any of it. He wasn't sure whether he wanted to be there anymore. Luckily one of the counselors pulled Devin aside and talked him through it. He ultimately told me he would be okay, so I gave him one last hug and left.

The staff at Camp Kesem are wonderful. They seem to have a special talent for relating to these children, helping them to feel better. The goal is for every kid to have an amazing time. Each day is filled with games and activities, and the counselors make sure to include the more timid kids, so they can join in the fun. I witnessed this firsthand, when I took both boys to the spring reunion the following year.

Otherwise it's a pretty normal camp. From what I understand, they don't actually spend much time talking about cancer. Instead, they focus on having lots of fun. However, there is a ceremony one night, for which the boys and girls separate. Each group forms a circle, and everybody gets to share the story of their loved one with cancer. I don't know any details about the ceremony itself, it's one of those special events you have to be part of to fully experience.

During Devin's first year he was known for playing his ocarina. The children aren't allowed any electronics, but they may bring a disposable camera, a journal, and a musical instrument. The ocarina was his favorite Christmas present that year – it is the same instrument Link has in the Zelda game series. He hadn't practiced for a while, but took it to camp anyway. Once there he played it constantly, even though he only knew a few Legend of Zelda songs. Amazingly, he figured out the theme to Harry Potter by ear at camp. Everyone loved it, and his unit mates managed to talk him into participating in the talent show. I wish I could have been there to see him perform for an audience that size. He played the songs he knew, and a counselor told me, he got a raucous, standing ovation. We could not have been more proud of him.

The following year Kayden got to attend camp as well, though he still barely made the age cut. He celebrated his 6th birthday *at* Camp Kesem. It was at a different location that time, so the boys got to enjoy new activities, like a zip line and a blob. Jenn was already gone then, but I followed along on their Facebook page. It was exciting to see pictures of Kayden on the zip line, or the kids swimming in a lake. Devin did not perform at the talent show that year, but Kayden did. Relatives were able to watch on a video. The audio wasn't great, but we could tell he was doing a cat hand-puppet show with his little buddies. It looked like they had a blast. When I went to pick up the boys, I got to hear the inside scoop. Kayden was known as Catster – another name I had suggested, because he is so obsessed with cats, he wants to be one. During meal times, after he finished eating, he would walk around and talk to random people. He also dab danced constantly to wild cheers. Every camper was given an award, personalized, and drawn onto a paper plate. Devin's read "Best Bear Hugger", and Kayden's was "Mr. Popular". I loved both.

After camp the boys got along much better. I can't express in words what Camp Kesem does for them, but it's incredible. When Devin went the first time, he returned more like his old self, before cancer struck our family. It only lasted until Kayden came back from his grandmother's house, but nonetheless, having the old Devin back for a bit had been touching and bittersweet. The next year, when both of them were home again, they were back to being good friends for the first time in a long while. It's not a perfect harmony, but they still continue to get along better than they did before they ever went to camp.

Kids lose special rituals they shared with the sick parent. I previously mentioned Jenn comparing their hands and feet to hers. Grief literature states that a good way to help children cope after a parent has died, is to carry on some of those traditions in their stead. Therefore I started having the boys hold up their hands and feet to mine – it was tradition they had with Jenn. I wasn't sure what other routines they had, so I asked if there was anything they used to do with mom that we didn't. They couldn't think of much, but Devin listed "Hang Out

Time", so we restructured the night time routine to include ten minutes of hanging out time, during which we talk about whatever comes to mind, big or small.

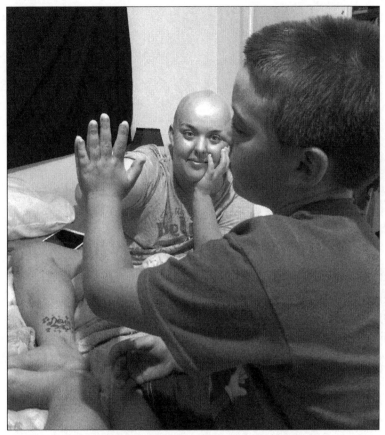

Jenn's ritual of comparing hands and feet.

These efforts payed off. It warmed my heart when Devin said to me one night, while I was giving him a hug, "The way you're hugging me reminds me of how mom used to hug me."

"Oh really?" I responded, "That's good. I always wondered how to give Mom Hugs." I continued to hold him like that for a while, letting him soak in the remembrance of his mom's embrace.

Then he stated, "You know dad, you're kind of like a mom and a dad." He immediately added, "Uh, I'm not saying you're like a girl or anything."

"I know, buddy. I know what you mean. I'm happy to hear you say that. I'm trying really hard to be like a mom and a dad at the same time."

"Well, you're doing a great job!" Those words meant the whole world to me.

Helping your children cope is tough. You're never sure if you're being too hard or too soft. My confidence plummeted, because I didn't know if anything I was doing was the best course of action in any given situation.

What makes it extra difficult is that I can't relate to what they're going through. Both of my parents are still alive, they love me and are proud of me. They did get divorced, so I can maybe kind of imagine what it's like to not have one of them present. Then again, even when I was living alone with my mom at Devin's age, my dad kept in touch on a weekly basis. I certainly never had to see one of my parents slowly get sicker and ultimately die.

I let them cry, and held them. I often told the boys, "It's okay to not be okay. It's okay to be sad. It's okay to be angry. It's normal because of what we're going through." I explained to them that people are like balloons, and emotions are like air, and if you don't let the air out before it's too late, you'll explode. Like adults, they needed a way to vent their feelings. After they had the chance to cry or express their anger, they could go back to whatever their new normal was. It might not have been their old normal, but at least it was a state of relative calm.

I've always had faith in the boys. I knew my kids had good hearts, and they would end up being okay. It was on me to not screw that up. My biggest concern was, if the depression pulled me so far down that they would essentially lose me, too, it could break them beyond repair. Thankfully, my boys properly mourned and adapted to their new lives like grief rock stars.

Chapter 8

Bucket List

"Somebody should tell us, right at the start of our lives, that we are dying. Then we might live life to the limit, every minute of every day. Do it! I say. Whatever you want to do, do it now! There are only so many tomorrows."

– POPE PAUL VI

AFTER JENN HAD processed the terminal diagnosis, and understood her remaining time was extremely limited, she realized the many things we wouldn't get to do together, as a couple and as a family. So she created a bucket list:

1. Take the boys to Disney World

2. Go on a second honeymoon

3. Appear on The Ellen Show

4. Meet Eric Whitacre

5. Meet the band Bayside

Jenn innocently published it on Twitter, and the response was overwhelming. Within a few days, Eric Whitacre, a world renowned classical music composer, tweeted to her, "I will personally make sure number 4 happens!" Jenn's response was, "Eric Whitacre just tweeted me, and he's going to meet me. What is my life right now?!"

Soon after Bayside tweeted something along the same lines. Meanwhile, family members and followers were busy working connections, pulling strings, and pooling resources to arrange a trip to Disney World, as well as a second honeymoon.

Jenn's avid followers on social media started a Facebook group called "Coopdizzle's Army," which quickly amassed over two hundred members. Their mission was to make the bucket list a reality, with the main focus on The Ellen Show. All two hundred plus members of the Coopdizzle Army sent e-mails and letters, recommending Jenn as a guest.

We were in disbelief, this was all happening so fast.

We didn't hear from Bayside again for a while, but Jenn started to develop a friendship with Eric Whitacre over Twitter. If you've never heard his music, I highly recommend it. As a band nerd, I was introduced to arrangements of his famous choir pieces in high school and college. I exposed Jenn to him while still in college, by showing her his first couple of Virtual Choir projects on YouTube. Introducing her to Whitacre's music was the initial step, which led Jenn to getting to know his music, some of his inner circle, and then the man himself.

Virtual Choir is a global project by Eric Whitacre, who first posts the parts to one of his pieces, plus a video of him conducting it. Then people around the world record videos of themselves singing it. After that, a patient soul edits all the videos together, creating the Virtual Choir. Jenn sang in a choir in high school, and had quickly fallen in love with it.

Back when we were living in the apartment, in our second year of marriage, she pitched the idea to me to submit videos for the next VC project. But one day, VC 3.0 was released on YouTube – we had missed it! A few years later, during my second year of teaching, a choir friend of mine posted to Facebook that he had just in time submitted his video for VC 4.0. We freaked out, quickly looked up the website, only to discover that the deadline for entry was hours away. I hastily grabbed Devin's cheap electric keyboard, we printed off parts, and I helped Jenn learn her part by playing it while she sang along. Once she had the gist of it, I went to another room to learn my part while she continued practicing. We each did a few takes and submitted our best ones. They were far from perfect, but they got in! Virtual Choir 4.0 is a gorgeous video, and the music has the power to teleport you to another realm. It's truly a beautiful experience. Although we could never find our faces among the ocean of people from all over the world, our names were in the credits, and it was an incredible feeling to have been part of something so epic.

Another VC related project came several months later. This was still before Jenn had cancer. Disney was inspired by Virtual Choir and had contracted Whitacre to write a holiday-inspired piece to be performed by singers of their choosing as part of one of their water light shows. The regular Virtual Choir accepts all submissions, but this one was different in that Eric Whitacre didn't have any control over it. You had to be selected by Disney's people, and there were a limited number of spots.

I brought out the old keyboard once again to help Jenn learn her part, this time well in advance. Jenn had also found a practice track one of the Virtual Choir Friends had posted in the community. She practiced at home, in the car, whenever and wherever she had the chance. For weeks, she worked her butt off to perfect it. Finally, the day of submissions had arrived, and we began the recording process. She did numerous takes, each with its own flaws. No matter how hard she tried, she just couldn't get "the one." Eventually, her voice started wearing out, her takes getting worse, so we decided to call it and chose the best one to submit, hoping she would make the cut.

She was accepted. Jenn was stoked. Making the Disney Virtual Honor Choir was one of her proudest achievements. Sadly, we weren't able to go to Disney to see it in action. The best we could do was watch low-resolution cell phone videos of it. But Jenn was ecstatic. She bragged to people that she was, "Disney Approved," and had a t-shirt made stating those exact words.

This plunged Jenn deeper into Virtual Choir Friends, which is a community filled with the most caring, empathetic and compassionate people you could ever meet.

Going back to right after Jenn had published her bucket list, it just so happened that a few of our VC Friends were in Eric Whitacre's inner circle. When they saw Jenn's tweet, they brought it to his attention, thus his response to her, "I will personally make sure number 4 happens." Later on, he sent her a private message, and after that they kept in touch until her death.

Some kind, local followers shared Jenn's story with their kids, who were Disney Vacation Club members. They agreed to hook us up with a two bedroom suite for a week in Saratoga Springs at Disney World. Jenn's followers dropped by one day to tell us the good news. Later on, their children also visited us to share all their insider tips. We were beyond excited. My brain was overloaded with all the information. If you've never been on a Disney vacation before, there is a lot to know if you want to get the most out of your trip. You don't have to, of course, but in my opinion it's far more enjoyable and less stressful, when you do a bit of planning ahead of time.

I am sorry to say, I cannot recall who got us the park tickets. It may have been that couple, or possibly another one of Jenn's followers. I'll blame that on my "trauma brain." The tickets were awesome, though. They included the park hopper option, which meant we could bounce between all four of the parks whenever we wanted to. If you ever go to Disney for a vacation, pay the extra money for that option, it is well worth it. One of Jenn's aunts, using her frequent flyer miles, bought the plane tickets for Jenn, Cindy, the boys, and myself.

Of course, we had hyped up the Disney trip as much as possible to our kids. I'd heard an incredible Disney story from a guest speaker at work. His family returned for a break from the park one day, and as they walked down the hall they heard the TV in their room blaring. Concerned, they entered their room to find their son's Buzz Lightyear and Woody dolls propped up on the pillow with a bag of popcorn, a couple of open soda cans, and the TV remote right in front of them. The son freaked out and yelled, "Dad! They were alive... and we ruined it!" When he questioned the management about it, hoping to repay whoever serviced their room that day, the manager simply said, "There's no need to. It's part of our mission, to create magic whenever the opportunity arises." I left out this last part but told the main story to my kids as an example of how there's "real magic" at Disney World. Devin was skeptical. He had stopped believing in magic and Santa Clause too early. We hoped this trip would give him the chance to reclaim some of his childhood, even if only for a brief time.

In June of 2015, we set off to Disney World for our great bucket list adventure. It was the boys' first time on an airplane. Both of them were pretty scared. Actually, Devin was more afraid, and his fear rubbed off on Kayden. Once we were in the air, Kayden adjusted much faster than Devin did. It reminded me of my first plane ride to visit my dad in Arizona.

We arrived in Orlando a little after lunch and rushed to catch our bus, the Disney Magical Express. They play Disney cartoons and trivia as well as preview the parks during the hour long ride to your resort. I quickly felt sold on the whole "Disney magic" thing. We were suckered in by the hype videos before we reached our hotel.

At the resort, however, we ran into the first of several bumps in our trip. I had no idea you could check into your room before your arrival, so naturally, we went to the front desk to get our keys. We were all exhausted from sleeping little and waking up early. Jenn and Cindy were especially worn out, and ready to get to our room. We had reserved scooters for them, which were thankfully ready to go. But our room, which was supposed to be ready by four o'clock, wouldn't be ready for another hour and a half. So, we sat around with nothing to do and nowhere to rest.

There was another major issue. We had been under the impression that a meal plan was included in our package.

Wrong. We had no meal plan and hadn't budgeted for it. Luckily, we did have extra money thanks to donations from Jenn's followers. The manager at the front desk sympathized with our situation, as well as the bucket list story, and gave me a large discount on their medium meal plan. It ended up being more than enough food for us.

We finally made it to our suite. It was nice, spacious, and an excellent place to retreat. The kids turned the TV to one of the Disney channels, and we all fell in love with the new Mickey Mouse cartoons. Things were getting back on track.

From the moment we had told the boys about going to Disney World, the most important item on Kayden's To-Do List was meeting Mickey Mouse. "I'm going to give him a high five, and a fist bump, and a hug!" He bothered us about it constantly. The day we arrived at the resort, he said, sadly, "Where's Mickey Mouse? I don't think he's here."

"No, Mickey lives in the Magic Kingdom part of Disney World. But don't worry, we're going there tomorrow!"

Waking up the next day, the only thing on Kayden's mind was meeting Mickey Mouse. So that was the first item on our agenda. As soon as you walk into the Magic Kingdom in Orlando, off to one side is a theater where you can meet Mickey and Tinkerbell. Devin thought Tinkerbell was hot, so he wanted to see her. I took Kayden to find Mickey while Jenn and Cindy went with Devin to look for Tinkerbell.

After standing in line for an eternity – far longer than the indicated wait time, we got to be in the same room. I held Kayden up so he could watch other families interact with him.

His eyes widened. He was star struck. The Mickey you meet at Disney World's Magic Kingdom is special, and very cool, because he talks and interacts with you. His mouth moves, and he can blink. Kayden was speechless, staring in fascination.

When it was our turn, his mood changed to one of survival. Suddenly he was scared to be close to Mickey. I suppose a giant, talking mouse would be strange to any four-year-old. Mickey did the best he could to interact. He pretended to be shy, too, but it wasn't working. Kayden stayed behind me, and fought back the tears. I went ahead and got Mickey to sign his book, then held Kayden for a picture. *I* hugged Mickey, and it was awesome. I felt bad for Kayden, though.

Devin had a wonderful experience meeting Tinkerbell. He told me how they went down a hallway, and it seemed enchanting, because the further down the hallway they went, it felt like they were gradually shrinking down to fairy size. In his picture, he's blushing hardcore. I love it.

So next we went on a ride we had "fast passed," Peter Pan's Flight. Devin's adrenaline from encountering Tinkerbell had worn off. As he looked around the park, he observed, "Dad, I don't see any magic around here."

"Be patient, buddy. I bet we'll see some before the trip is over." Sure enough, they both felt spellbound on Peter Pan's Flight. The little things added up to a marvelous experience, from the way the operators sprinkle fairy dust on the lap bar to secure it, to the moment we were flying over London at night, traveling to Neverland. The boys were in awe, and after that, had a much better time. When you get there and stand in line forever before meeting a character, it's anti-climactic. That ride enhanced everyone's mood.

The boys started *finding* Disney magic all over the place. I didn't have to do anything other than say, "Wow, that's cool!" If they asked me how something worked, I would just say, "I don't know. I guess it's Disney Magic!" Kayden was an easy sell, but Devin got hooked after the parade, right as the light and fireworks show was starting. On a musical cue, Tinkerbell flew through the air and disappeared somewhere near the castle. Devin's mouth was agape.

"There really is magic here!" he said with the kind of excitement I hadn't seen from him since before Jenn had cancer.

It was amazing. Here was an eight-year-old child for whom all magic was dead, even the mystery of Christmas, believing in it again. And the most wonderful thing about that week at Disney was how the boys got to just be kids again. I can't put a price on that. The timing was perfect, as it was our last chance to do that for Devin before he was too old and cynical.

The trip was just as miraculous for Kayden. When we were at Epcot the second day, he still shied away from all of the characters, but then observed Devin interacting with Chip and Dale. Those two were hilarious. One was messing with Devin while the other was signing his book, then they passed it over, and the other one gave him high fives. They ribbed him a little bit, and Devin ribbed them back. It was fun to watch, and Kayden noticed. After that, he started talking about how he wanted to meet Mickey again, how it would be different next time, and that if he met Chip and Dale, he would do it the way Devin did.

Sure enough, by day four he came out of his shell and interacted with characters. We went back to Epcot and had dinner at a place where they wandered around and interacted with guests. The first to come up to us was Pluto. Kayden was shy at first, but he reached out and petted Pluto's nose. Then he showed Pluto a Pluto doll we had bought earlier, and of course, the "real" Pluto loved that. Next came Chip and Dale, and Kayden was a little braver this time, giving them high fives and poking their noses. Finally came Mickey Mouse. Kayden warmed up to Mickey by showing him the Pluto doll, which Mickey liked. Then Kayden reached out and gave him a big hug! Jenn was quick with the camera! Kayden sat down until I said, "Wait, aren't you going to give him a high five and a fist bump, too?" So of course, he did, and I was glad. I didn't want him to have any regrets.

Kayden hugging Mickey Mouse!

Kayden had always been terrified of the pool. At Disney Kayden practically became a fish and fell in love with swimming. He even built up the courage to go down water slides, do cannonballs, and swim around on his own. We had never been able to get him to do that. There was something about this place.

The boys got along much better that week. We still had our moments, but overall, they were acting like friends and being kids again. It was the first time I had seen them this way since Jenn had been diagnosed.

Jenn and I enjoyed a date night in the Magic Kingdom. Because we were staying at a resort, we got access to "Extra Magic Hours." We took advantage of those by going to Hollywood Studios and on the Hollywood Tower of Terror – now my all-time favorite ride, screaming our heads off. The Magic Kingdom felt special. Jenn and I did all the cheesy stuff. We went on the Magic Carpet Ride, rode the carousel, and even met some of the princesses, including Ariel, who had always been her favorite. Our sadness did cast a shadow over the evening though. We were only there because Jenn was dying. But we did our best to put those thoughts aside and enjoy being together in "The Most Magical Place on Earth."

Jenn's favorite moment happened at Epcot. There is an aquarium with all kinds of amazing sea life, including a few dolphins. Jenn *loved* dolphins. Knowing it was a long shot, Jenn found a cast member who was providing trivia facts to visitors. She explained that she was dying, loved dolphins, and wondered if there was any way she could get close to one of them. The cast member hopped on her radio and took a few minutes to look into it. Apparently a couple of the dolphins were sick, so they weren't allowing visitors, although they did say it is possible to arrange for a swim with dolphins under normal circumstances and with advanced notice.

What they did do is involve our family in the dolphin show happening later that day. She told us when to come back, and we left. I can't remember where I ran off to, but there was something I really wanted to do before the dolphin show. I hustled back only to catch the very end of my family motioning the dolphins to do tricks. I missed it, but all three of them were beaming, especially Jenn. She didn't get to swim with dolphins, but got to communicate with them, and she was thrilled beyond words. I was grateful for that.

Family picture after the dolphin show.

We managed to meet some friends as well. A Virtual Choir friend, who had worked with Eric Whitacre, met us for dinner our first night. He brought out his laptop and showed Jenn a special video. Over a dozen VC Friends had gotten together and recorded a custom arrangement he had written of "Wind Beneath My Wings." In addition to harmony changes, he tweaked the lyrics to personalize them for Jenn. We were blown away by the kindness and compassion of this group. The video is still on YouTube. You can find it by searching for "Wings for Jenny."

We got together with one of Jenn's Fitocracy friends for dinner at the Rainforest Café in Downtown Disney, which is now called Disney Springs, on a different evening.

Truly, it was an incredible trip for all of us, one we will remember for the rest of our lives. Bucket list item number one – check.

Over the next several months, Jenn kept in touch with Eric Whitacre. We were working with his people to figure out the details of a meet up. We hadn't heard anything from Bayside, but they had announced they were playing at a festival in the Dallas/Ft. Worth area, which happened to fall on the same weekend Eric Whitacre was going to conduct a concert there. We chose that opportunity to meet him, and were hoping we might get to meet Bayside, too.

Saturday, March nineteenth, we went to the SoWhat? Music Festival in Grand Prairie, Texas. Although Bayside was slotted to play at a later time, we decided to hang out all day and check out other bands. Plus, we were supposed to talk to a festival coordinator. Jenn's story had spread to the people running the event, and they had agreed to do what they could to help us meet Bayside.

Although we enjoyed listening to the other groups, whether or not Jenn would get to meet her all-time favorite band – next to Queen – was a looming cloud over her head. She was following their tweets, and we heard one piece of bad news after another. First, their flight was delayed. They managed to book a private plane to get to the festival, which was good news. Then the flight took longer than expected. Jenn occasionally tweeted updates to her followers, tagging the band, reiterating how badly she wanted to meet them.

The festival coordinators said they would try to get us time with the band before they went on, but that window eventually closed when they tweeted about having just landed and being rushed to the venue. They barely made it on stage in time.

Bayside sounded amazing. Even so, Jenn couldn't help but cry. It was her first time seeing them in concert, probably her only chance to meet them, and it wasn't going to happen. She felt so close. I advised her to try to brush it off and enjoy the show, but I understood why that was difficult. They did play our wedding song, *Landing Feet First,* though, and we got to dance to it.

Afterward, the band went backstage. Bayside had responded to Jenn's bucket list tweet several months earlier, so she took a chance. She saw their merchandise vendor, who asked how she had liked the show. Jenn said they sounded amazing, but that she was very sad. Tears flowed as she expressed her anguish about never having another chance, that they had been her favorite band for ten years, and how she just wanted to meet them before she died. The vendor tried to comfort her and encouraged her to hang on, to let him see if he could get them to come out and say, "Hi."

We waited in the chilly wind for several minutes to see what the verdict would be, when Jack, the lead guitarist, made his way over to the fence separating the crowd from the backstage area. Jack is an awesome guy. He was super nice and funny.

"We saw your tweets!" he told us, "We really wanted to bring you guys back before the show, but then our schedule got so crazy!" This meant a lot to Jenn. She felt like she had been seen.

Next was Nick, the bass guitarist. A minute or two later, Chris and Anthony, the guitarist and lead singer, respectively, came out together. Jenn doesn't normally get star struck, but she did when she saw Anthony. Becky was with us that day, standing back to take pictures.

Jenn with Bayside.

I chatted with the other band members, telling them how much I enjoyed their music and thanking them for it. Then I stepped back, and Becky took a picture of Jenn with the whole band. She was on cloud nine that night. Bucket list item number five – check.

After the concert, we joined one of my all-time best friends – and best man at our wedding – and his girlfriend at the Cheesecake Factory for fantastic company and a delicious dinner. Then we retreated to our hotel room. We had wanted to go to bed early, as we had a breakfast date with Eric Whitacre, but it was a little difficult because we were still feeling the rush of meeting Bayside.

When we woke up we were exhausted, especially Jenn, but equally excited to meet the world renowned classical composer Eric Whitacre for breakfast. We arrived on time, but he managed to beat us. All three of us were star struck when we saw him. Eric stood up with the biggest smile I have ever seen in my life, then gave Jenn a great, big hug. Fun fact about Eric Whitacre – he's a *great* hugger.

The conversation was a bit slow at first, but as everyone became more comfortable the ice broke, and it felt like a chat among good friends. After providing the obligatory praise and gratitude for his music, we mostly talked about our cancer journey. He was fascinated by all the hardship we had faced, and how well we were managing to cope, Jenn in particular. We asked about his life and family, and learned a lot about him, but he did a good job of redirecting the conversation back toward us.

After we had finished eating, our waitress said we were welcome to stay and should not feel a rush to leave. She may have regretted that later. We all figured breakfast with a guy as busy as Eric Whitacre might be an hour, maybe an hour and a half if we were lucky. Eventually we realized we had been talking for two and a half hours. Had we had more time, we could have easily chatted for twice that long. We parted ways with pictures and more of his legendary hugs, then went home, completely stoked about the epic weekend we had just wrapped up. Bucket List item number four – check.

Jenn with Eric Whitacre after breakfast.

After Bayside and Eric Whitacre, Jenn set her sights on going to more concerts and meeting more bands. On May ninth of that year, Jenn got together with Pentatonix. They're an incredibly talented a cappella group, complete with a beatboxer to add a modern sound to their performances. They became famous through YouTube for their arrangements of popular songs, but they've since released a number of original tracks as well.

Sadly, due to STAAR Testing – the standardized, government mandated test in Texas schools – I wasn't able to go. You can't get a substitute to cover you for these, because only those who have gone through the proper training may administer a test. Most band directors don't even have to do it, we normally get put on bathroom duty or something like that. I was just unlucky in that regard, so Jenn had to take the boys without me. But I will share what they told me.

Jenn's friend Stephanie picked her and the boys up. By then, Jenn didn't feel comfortable driving herself anymore, much less the kids, so Stephanie drove them to Austin, where they met up with Becky.

They arrived early so they could go to the sound check, which was a perk of their VIP tickets. Afterward, all VIP ticket holders got in line to meet each of the band members, and get their VIP passes autographed. Jenn and her entourage were at the end of the queue, but Jenn still caught the attention of each band member, sharing her story and taking the opportunity to educate them about breast cancer. Jenn gave the female vocalist an awareness bracelet, which she later wore on stage. She made it a point to tell the guys in the group that, yes, men can get breast cancer. Because they were at the end of the line, Jenn had the full band's attention for a few moments. Though soon they had to leave to get ready for the show.

When Jenn and her group returned for the concert, Jenn struggled with a set of stairs. Her ticket wasn't specifically for a handicapped seat, and that set of stairs proved to be a painful reminder of her increasing limitations. Fortunately, a few handicapped seats were available. Kayden sat on her lap in that seat, away from the others, while Devin sat with Stephanie, Becky and another longtime friend of Jenn's.

Although the boys had to wear ear plugs, they both loved the show. It was their first live concert. Jenn said Kayden's eyes were wide the entire time, and his mouth was agape. I can testify to how much the boys enjoyed the experience, because for weeks afterward, all they wanted to listen to in the car was Pentatonix, and they sang along together. They bonded over it, which made me happy. Plus, Devin has a great singing voice, and I hadn't heard him use it much since Jenn's initial diagnosis.

Jenn loved going to concerts, and I was grateful she had the chance to share this love with our sons, if only once. I was bummed out I couldn't go, but I hope it's a trip the boys will always remember.

A couple of months later, in the summer of 2016, we once again packed our bags and got on a plane, this time to Disneyland in California.

The trip was facilitated by one of Jenn's followers, who had referred her to Ally's Wish, which is a charity dedicated to providing one last wish to young, terminally ill moms with small children. For months Jenn had been going back and forth by phone and e-mail with their coordinator to get everything organized. The initial plan was to send us to Disney World. "We've already been to Disney World," Jenn explained, "But what about Disneyland?" Ally's Wish made it happen for us. It wasn't part of Jenn's Bucket List, but it was a very welcome gift and a much needed reprieve.

We wouldn't be staying at a Disney resort this time, but a Hyatt in Orange County. Our three-day park tickets with park hopper option left us with two extra days in California, so we planned on going whale spotting. We figured we could hang out at the hotel to enjoy the amenities the rest of the time. We tried to save money for the trip, but it wasn't easy. Thankfully, Jenn's followers donated to help with food and gas for the rental car.

I loved Los Angeles the moment we arrived. It's a beautiful city, and the people are much nicer than I had expected. While driving on the freeway to Orange County, I was nervous about the legendary LA traffic. Sure, it was cramped and very slow, but otherwise laid back and friendly. People worked together in sharing the road, letting other drivers cut in front of them as needed. The entire week there, I only remember seeing one reckless driver, though motorcyclists were a different story. Still, we had a great introduction to the culture in California.

Jenn managed to join us for the first day at the park. We started with the Magic Kingdom, though Mickey Mouse wasn't at the front of the park this time, so we saved meeting him for later. The heat quickly became oppressive, and before lunchtime

Jenn and the boys were in a bad mood. They settled down once everyone got to eat, but after only a few kiddy rides, Jenn was exhausted. She went back to the room while I stayed with the boys for a while before our afternoon break.

The whole week turned out to be like that for Jenn. She couldn't join us for a second day at the park, again leaving me in single dad mode as I took the boys and enjoyed all the children's entertainment both the Magic Kingdom and California Adventures had to offer. It was still fun, but Jenn's absence cast a shadow over the trip. At least Devin and Kayden weren't as affected by it as I was, so I made a conscious decision to enjoy the parks with their beautiful landscaping and artistry surrounding us.

Toon Town and Radiator Springs were our favorites. Mickey and Minnie live in Toon Town, an area with every trope from all of the classic cartoons to walk around in and explore. Devin's imagination flourished. He saw a mail bin and tried to open it just to see if he could. When he did, the mailbox talked to him.

"Hey, you gonna put some mail in here or what?" it said in a thick Boston accent. We all smiled in surprise. He opened it again, and it said, "Man, people sure do like to mail stuff!" Each time, it said something different. In the last one, we heard two voices talking about how much they loved reading people's mail. This inspired us to discover what other Easter eggs might be hidden here. We opened a box labeled, "Spare Train Parts" and heard a locomotive engine. You could pick up a phone and Donald Duck started talking to you. It was unbelievably cool. Toon Town had come alive, with all of the old cartoons from my youth flooding my memory. The jail had flimsy bars you could easily move and walk through. A sign read, "Caution, Safe

Falling Zone" and sure enough, a safe was lying in the street, having cracked the pavement around it. The entire place is a marvel of imagination and detail.

Radiator Springs was equally great. We went at night and rode the two kiddy rides, which were a lot of fun for me, too. Then we explored the town, complete with neon lights and surrounded by canyons. It looked exactly like the movie. At the center of town, a car named DJ drove down the street with a posse of female dancers and started a party. I couldn't get Devin to join, but Kayden and I danced together. Then we saw Tow Mater coming down the street, escorted by a human security detail. Kayden's eyes lit up, "Dad, look, it's the real Mater!"

"Let's go follow him!" I said. We walked behind him as he said hello to people in the crowd. We ended up back at the Cozy Cone, where Lightning McQueen was taking pictures with people.

"Hi buddy, I guess it's my turn!" Mater said to McQueen.

"Alright, Mater. Have fun! Ka-chow!" McQueen replied, and then he followed Mater's human escorts back to wherever they had come from.

I've never felt as immersed in another world at any theme park, as I had at the Disney parks in California.

We got in line to take a picture with Tow Mater, and later on, we got one with Lightning McQueen. We ate ice cream at the Cozy Cone and explored the Doc Hudson museum, where you can see all the Piston Cups on display. It was truly fantastic.

That night, after the boys were asleep, Jenn and I faced a dilemma. The boys wanted so badly to check out Legoland while we were in California. They had watched videos of it, and all I could say is that we would try. Once I found out the ticket prices, though, I wasn't so sure. They cost more than one hundred dollars per person. We debated whether or not to do it. It was going to be tight money wise, but ultimately Jenn thought I should take them after the whale watch the next day. After all, when would we be in California again? Possibly never. If there was one thing we had learned through cancer, it's that you have to live life while you can, and not wait to do the fun stuff, especially if the opportunity presents itself.

The next day was whale spotting day. It's hard to describe what an awe-inspiring experience it is. It's something you have to do in person to appreciate. Video can't do it justice. Once we got onto the ocean, I was surprised at how adept the captain was at finding whales. Seeing one close up when they're underwater is humbling, but once they come up for air, it's exhilarating. The sheer size of whales is unfathomable until you stand close to one. The awe I felt reminded me of the time my dad took me to the Grand Canyon in Arizona as a teenager, but more exciting. This was easily Jenn's favorite part of the trip.

The traffic on our way there hadn't been bad. We had expected to be on the boat for an hour and a half, but it ended up being close to three hours. By the time we left, traffic was terribly slow. We had to stop on the way to the hotel to get something to eat, which meant we got a late start on getting to Lego Land. A very late start. It took a couple of hours from Orange County to north of San Diego, Carlsbad. We rushed, but by the time we reached the park, they were only open for another hour.

And that was a real shame, because I quickly realized that this place was a lot more fun for the boys than the Disney parks. All the rides are designed for kids, and while they're not necessarily top quality – the vessels barely operating on the boat ride for example, they were highly entertaining. Since the boys were having fun, so was I. We managed to spend another hour at the park by slowly walking back to the entrance and stopping in a couple of souvenir shops. Then we had another two-hour drive back to Orange County.

The last day at the parks was emotional. In chapter five I had written about the traumatic event where Jenn thought she was going to die in a hotel room, and this was when that happened. But the rest of that night was wonderful. Jenn joined us in the parks. We showed her Radiator Springs, went to take photos with Goofy – Jenn's favorite Disney character – before going to the Magic Kingdom for fireworks and a light show. Having her there made us incredibly happy It was a great end to a mostly fun week, despite our circumstances. Like the Pentatonix concert, this may not have been on Jenn's Bucket List, but when you're going through something so difficult, you're eager to take any opportunities you can. We were grateful to have been able to make one last, big family trip.

Later that summer, Jenn and I went on our second honeymoon, thanks to Jenn's aunt, who had graciously set us up with a hotel suite in South Padre Island for a week. We managed to scrape enough money together to cover gas, food for a week, extra cash for souvenirs, and a few tourist attractions we had read about. It was exciting to have an entire week to ourselves, and at such a beautiful location.

Upon arrival we immediately sat on the balcony to enjoy the sounds of the ocean.

Jenn and I bought groceries so we wouldn't have to spend a lot of money eating out. It was the first time I had cooked dinner in several years. Right then and there I decided it was time to stop feeding my family fast food, and prepare healthy, home-cooked meals instead. It was a turning point.

We did eat out at least once a day, though. We *had* to try the local seafood. There was a pirate-themed restaurant on the mainland. Jenn loved pirates. She often set her Facebook language to pirate just for fun, so that place was perfect.

I got a massage while Jenn got her nails done one day, and the next we went dolphin spotting. I tried para-sailing, which was incredible. What an amazing view.

My favorite activity was a romantic dinner cruise. We set out at around sunset, on a small boat, with several other couples. The food was delicious. Dinner was fajitas with chicken, steak, shrimp, and all the fixings. As we ate and cruised on the water, a crew member played his guitar and sang. I spent most of my time cuddling with Jenn, although we also chatted with the other passengers. Jenn never missed an opportunity to spread awareness for breast cancer or promote her social media. Good food, great music, wonderful company, beautiful surroundings – it all made for an amazing evening.

Jenn and I on a romantic dinner cruise.

On our last day there, Jenn had enough energy to head to the beach. All she wanted was to feel the ocean water run over her feet. She soaked up the smell and taste of the air. I got brave and ventured out into the water. After I did, Jenn followed. She wanted to take turns to make sure her camera didn't get stolen. She didn't get as far out as I did before feeling nervous about her lack of strength. It was fun, but bittersweet. A common theme in all of our bucket list experiences.

It may sound like we did a lot, but we spent most of our time in the room. Jenn was in bed, often asleep. Sitting in the living room, where I was most comfortable, was too painful for her. Whenever she was awake, I made an effort to sit next to her, but I spent the majority of our second honeymoon alone in the living room or on the balcony, playing Minecraft on my laptop. At times I felt frustrated and bitter. Looking around at all the healthy couples and families, I wished that could be us. Most people honeymoon at South Padre to enjoy the beach and have tons of sex, and I envied them. I pushed those thoughts aside and enjoyed the time I did have with Jenn. There is no sense in wishing for the impossible. Besides, I was rarely lonely when she was asleep, thanks to my friends on the Diamond Society Minecraft server. Someone was always playing, which meant I had people to talk to.

Please don't think I am complaining. Overall, it was a wonderful week. I just had to temper my expectations. We enjoyed having that time to be together, to reconnect and create fun memories. Bucket List item number two – check.

We hadn't been home for long when the Texas Bandmasters Association Convention in San Antonio took place, which is a band director convention I attend every year. Jenn typically went with me, but didn't go the year before because she hadn't been healthy enough. This time she didn't care if she was feeling well or not – Eric Whitacre was going to be there, and they wanted to meet up again. He was giving a speech at the choir director's convention that ran parallel to the band one. He was also conducting the US Air Force Band of the West on two of his pieces. We hoped to be able to meet him at some point, but nothing was set in stone.

On the day of his speech we woke up early to make sure we got a front row seat in the convention hall. Eric saw us sitting there, flashed us his huge smile, and waved enthusiastically. Even this gesture was exciting. His speech was wonderful, filled with humor and insight.

Afterward, he waved us backstage. A lady acting as his security stopped us and explained that Mr. Whitacre was very busy and didn't have time to talk to the attendees. Jenn explained we were friends, and that he had waved us back. She looked at us skeptically. Fortunately, Eric came out from the backstage area to rescue us. The security lady seemed almost disappointed. There wasn't much time, but we chatted for a few minutes and tried to make plans for later. It was awesome to talk to him again, even for just a brief time. It felt like reconnecting with an old friend.

Fast forward to that night. The Air Force Band concert was the main event of the evening. We arrived at the Lila Cockrell Theater almost an hour early to get seats in the handicapped booth, a nice spot in the back center of the bottom floor. One of our Virtual Choir friends joined us there, as well as Becky, who lived close by. It was awesome to meet our VC friend in person. We killed some time by going live on Facebook until the concert began.

When Eric Whitacre was introduced, he walked out to the applause of a packed house of over 2,300 people. He started conducting *October*, which was the first piece of his I had performed as a high school senior. This music had introduced me to his work. It made me feel nostalgic and I reminisced about that band, the year we had had, and that concert, which had been the last time I performed with them before graduation.

The second piece he conducted was *Sleep*, which is an all-time favorite of mine. But before they started, they allowed a choir to come on stage. It was the Texas Choir Director's Association Director's Choir, comprised of several dozen vocal directors from across the state. They lined up on risers behind the Air Force Band of the West, then Eric returned to the stage to introduce the music.

Eric explained how the original choir version and the band arrangement were written in the same key so they could be performed together. I didn't know this, and I was very excited to hear it in this mixed setting. He provided interesting background information about the piece before saying something that would both exhilarate our group and break my heart.

"I would like to dedicate this piece to a very special woman. I believe she's in the audience tonight. Her name is Jennifer Cooper. She has been battling terminal breast cancer, and she is the most courageous woman I've ever met."

We were completely stunned. I had given up my seat to an elderly couple, so I was standing behind Jenn the entire concert with my hand on her shoulder. I leaned down to kiss her on the head and then kneeled behind her. Jenn had the biggest smile on her face. Becky and our VC Friend were ecstatic for her. Everyone was thrilled, including me, but I was also disheartened.

Sleep is a soothing composition of music making me feel as if I am drifting away, except for the build-up to its climax, which is packed with emotion and musical expression. Perhaps that section represents sleeplessness as thoughts race through your head. Listening, I reflected on the past again, only this time about the cancer journey. Everything we had been through flashed before my eyes as the song progressed. I tried to bring myself back to the present moment, but couldn't stay there. All of the happy experiences we'd shared, the great things Jenn had accomplished since being diagnosed also came up. We had been able to do so much I would've never experienced otherwise, but only because she was dying, and while it was exciting, it wasn't worth the cost. I remember thinking I may never be able to listen to that music again, or anything by Eric Whitacre, without crying. Then I heard it – the buildup.

I focused on holding back the tears, but with each rise from the choir, I felt my eyes welling up. This is why part of me wasn't delighted when Eric dedicated it to Jenn. I knew it would be emotionally devastating. Despite all the meditation, therapy, medications, and other efforts to put myself back together, I felt it all come undone through this performance. When the musical climax arrived, I lost it. Tears were gushing forth like a dam releasing its water reserve. I tried to at least weep silently. I knew this piece had a slow resolution, and if my emotions were running in tandem with the music, then perhaps they would gradually settle as well. Still, the damage had been done. My head was in a very dark place, bitter about what we were losing, afraid of the future awaiting me, angry and saddened that my sons would have to grow up without their mother. The grief hit me all at once, and I was a wreck.

After the music concluded, I excused myself. I needed to get out of there, so I could cry and grieve and not disturb the rest of the audience. Later that night, I met up with Jenn and a few other friends for drinks. I wrote about what had happened on my personal Facebook page, the response to which inspired me to start Coffee With Coop. We wanted to go to bed a little earlier than usual because Eric was speaking at another clinic in the morning, and Jenn, despite feeling exhausted, was eager to attend. Her cancer had other plans.

Jenn woke up the next morning, unable to breathe. Panic crept in, though I did my best to remain calm. I asked on social media for recommendations for a good hospital in town. While those came in, I had Jenn take her medications. She occasionally had been having trouble breathing due to the cancer on her diaphragm and in the lining of her lungs. Sometimes once the steroids started working, the symptoms abated, so we waited to see if her condition would improve. Half an hour went by with no change, so I made preparations to leave immediately. Jenn messaged Eric on Twitter to let him know we wouldn't make it to the clinic. The original plan had been to go to lunch together afterward, and Jenn was depressed that we wouldn't get to have any quality time with him. It was, after all, her last chance. I took her phone, got on her Twitter, and sent Eric a note to let him know which hospital we were going to, in case he had the chance to stop by before he left town. No pressure, of course.

We drove to a local hospital. By the time we arrived, Jenn was in agony, so they ran some tests and gave her "the good stuff" – morphine, probably – to reduce the pain. Soon Jenn was loopy and happy, and after a while, who walked in? Eric Whitacre, himself.

Eric's visit was a huge surprise and uplifting to both of us. For forty-five minutes he sat next to Jenn and talked to her, holding her hand. I stayed out of the way. I couldn't believe he had gone out of his way like that for us. Eventually, the staff came in to take Jenn away for chest imaging. I figured that would be Eric's cue to leave, but instead, he turned to me.

"I read what you wrote last night. It was beautiful," he said. I thanked him, and then we started chatting. To my surprise, he

191

stayed another forty-five minutes, and it was a wonderful, uplifting conversation. "I want to be Jenn's friend until she's gone, but you and me, I hope we can be friends for the rest of our lives." We exchanged contact information and pledged to keep in touch.

I still can't believe that I, a lowly, no-name band director, became friends with a world-famous composer whose music I love and admire. Was it worth losing Jenn? Of course not. But since we couldn't change her fate, we accepted and appreciated anything positive coming our way. In other good news, Jenn had pneumonia. For most people this would be bad news, but we were relieved her lung wasn't collapsed or filled with fluid. We left the hospital with Jenn feeling a bit loopy, but both of us in great spirits. If you didn't know who Eric Whitacre was before this, I hope you go and check out his music and maybe even support him in some way. I have never met a person as kind-hearted as he is.

Our adventures weren't quite over yet. Jenn continued to deteriorate, but she wanted to do as much as possible in the time she had left.

We saw Bayside again, in San Antonio. By this point, Jenn could hardly stand, mostly sitting in a wheelchair. We went to the sound check and said hello to the band. They played in an old warehouse that had been converted into a small concert venue. I worried Jenn wouldn't be able to see past the people standing in front of her, so I talked to an employee and managed to get us into an elevated roped off VIP area. Becky joined us, and we enjoyed the music. Sadly, Jenn was nodding off throughout the concert. She was angry about that, too. We tried to keep her awake, but couldn't.

Which brings us to the last hurrah, or what I refer to as the "Epic Weekend." Let me back up a bit.

Rewind about one year. Jenn was driving home from San Angelo when she heard a band called Twelve Foot Ninja on the radio. Their song had caught her ear, so she watched the music video online. Jenn loved it so much, she shared it on my Facebook timeline, without tagging the band or anything like that. She simply commented, "Just leaving this here for Christopher Charles Cooper."

A few days later, Twelve Foot Ninja commented on her post, "And did Christopher like it?" We were blown away. How often does a band do that?

You may not have heard of the group. They're a fusion metal band from Australia. Some metal-heads hear "Fusion Metal" and get a sour feeling in their stomach, but they're different. They do it extremely well. Their second album, *Outlier* won numerous awards in Australia. They've toured internationally, including the United States, and this past summer they opened for Disturbed on a tour of Australia. These guys are legit.

So Jenn responded, "....Yes. But how did you find this post?"

Naturally, their response was, "Because we're ninjas!"

It's a crazy coincidence, but the band's leader, Stevic, had just started watching Jenn's YouTube videos, so they discovered each other around the same time. Stevic found perspective in Jenn's story. Everything he was stressed out about seemed minuscule in comparison to what Jenn was dealing with. They became friends and kept in touch on Facebook.

What I'm going to say from here on out is going to sound unbelievable, but I promise, it's all true.

As Jenn and Stevic continued talking, Jenn added meeting Twelve Foot Ninja to her bucket list. She told him she wanted to meet them so badly, just once, before she died. He said they were working on it, but being an up-and-coming band meant their resources were limited. Months went by, and Jenn was stressed about dying before they would ever make it to the United States.

Then one day on Facebook, the band posted a flyer for a festival... in Texas, with the comment, "So yeah, it looks like we're doing this."

To which their US fans responded, "Why are you only doing one festival... and why in Texas?!" We were pretty sure we knew the reason. Within a few weeks, more stops in the US showed up on their schedule, but by then we had our tickets to their initial show.

"Don't even worry about buying VIP tickets," Stevic told Jenn, "We'll take care of all that." They wanted to get us backstage to hang out with them before their show. We were astounded and excited.

Then something significant to me happened. Minecon dates were announced. You could say attending Minecon was on my bucket list. The location was California, the same city we had gone to for Disneyland. The only problem? It was on the same weekend as the Twelve Foot Ninja concert.

We talked about it again and again. I wanted to go, but I didn't want to miss Twelve Foot Ninja. I tried to resign myself not to attend Minecon, but Jenn was insistent. She felt I deserved the trip for everything I had done for her during the cancer journey, and that I should get to cross something off of my bucket list, too. The festival the band was performing at was a multi-day event, but we didn't know which day they were on. Neither did the band at the time. So we decided I would try to snag a Minecon ticket, hoping they were playing on the first day. I would miss day 1 of Minecon, but make it for day 2, and if I was lucky, I'd also get to see the band. I was loving their music, too, and desperately wanted to experience them live. Unfortunately, we found out shortly before the trip that their performance was scheduled right as I would have to fly out of town. This made me want to stay, but again, Jenn insisted I go. I had been fortunate to get a scarce Minecon ticket, and there were Diamond Society friends whom I would finally see in person. It made sense to me that meeting these guys, whom I'd been gaming with for over a year, spent a lot of time venting to and gotten to know pretty well, was ultimately more important. Maybe one day I'll get another shot at seeing the Ninjas live.

And so, on September 23rd, 2016, the Epic Weekend began. We swung through San Angelo to pick up Jenn's friend Jeska, and then spent seven hours instead of the usual four on the road to Fort Worth. At least it was an enjoyable ride, but exhausting. For those of you not familiar with Texas, we drove nine hours and only got from Central Texas to East Texas. It's a big place.

Becky met us at the hotel the next morning as Jenn and Jeska were getting ready. From there we set out to the Texas Motor Speedway, where the concert was being held. Jenn had been given the cell phone number for the band's assistant, who met us in the parking area. He handed us each a "Band Member" pass, and as we approached the backstage area, he advised in his charming Australian accent, "Don't even look at the security guard. Just walk in like you own the place." We did just that.

Anticipation was already high, but it reached its climax as we walked past several tour buses before arriving at the Ninja's bus. Jenn was the first to go on. She lit up, and so did the band, when they met each other in person. It was an incredible feeling to witness this happening. Jenn hugged all of the band members. I'm more of a hand shaker if I don't know someone, so that's what I did, but soon we all sat down and chatted.

Jenn and Cindy had prepared a care package for the band. It consisted of snacks and different coffees only available in Texas. We had two or three bags full of stuff for them. It was fun to watch Jenn explain everything, and to see their reactions as the gifts just kept coming. It took several minutes to get through it all.

Jenn visiting Twelve Foot Ninja on their bus.

"Now I feel bad. You brought us all this cool stuff, and all we have are a few t-shirts," one of them commented.

Someone grabbed the t-shirts, and another band member instructed, "Make sure you hand it over to them *really slowly!*"

"Yeah, and make sure you read the tags!" another one said. I wish I could remember who said what, but it was just comedic how they were trying to draw out the giving of their gifts. We loved it, of course. They had two shirts for Jenn and a shirt for each of the boys. They ran off to get more merchandise, including shirts for Becky, Jeska, and myself, as well as hats for me and the boys.

The band autographed Devin's shirt, and when Kayden's shirt was getting passed around, I said, "You know, for Kayden, he'd probably rather you draw a cat on it or something like that. He's obsessed with cats."

"A cat, eh?" Stevic said. His brain was working on something special.

"Stevic is the man for that. He's the artist in the group," another band member commented. Stevic got to work, and a few minutes later unveiled his masterpiece. The shirt depicted two ninja swords pointed toward each other, crossing in the middle. I had been thinking of a small stick figure cat or something simple, but this was incredible. Stevic had drawn a huge cartoon cat from the waist up, reaching up and clasping one sword in each hand, wearing a bandanna to denote it as a ninja cat. We were blown away.

We had interesting and deep conversations after that. The band members were all inspired by Jenn. The lead singer, Kin, made an especially poignant observation about Jenn maintaining her sense of humor and joking about death, and how through that, she was staring death in the face and laughing at it as a way to cope. I thought that was extremely cool and poetic.

We took a bunch of pictures with the band. Jenn remembered me telling her how I regretted not getting a picture with Bayside the first time we met them, so she made sure I got a group picture this time. I'm so glad I did.

Then things got a bit hectic for me. It was time for Jenn to take her medication, but she had forgotten rather important ones at the hotel room. I was supposed to leave for the airport in a little over an hour, and we were about half an hour away from the hotel. Jenn asked me to go, so I rose to the occasion. I said my goodbyes to the band and dashed to the car. I got to the hotel and back as fast as I could, my heart racing the entire way, trying to get Jenn her meds as soon as possible and also not wanting to miss my flight to Minecon.

I made it back just in time. The band was elsewhere when I returned, but the girls had stayed on the bus to avoid the heat. The band wanted to spend the entire day with them – how cool is that? I said my goodbyes to Jenn and her friends and took an extra few moments with Jenn to wish her an awesome day. What I didn't know then is that it would be the last good day she would ever have.

It was a mad dash back to the car and another fast drive to the airport. I made it just in time to grab a bite to eat and hop on the plane. A few hours later I was back in California for the first time since Disneyland.

A short bus ride took me to my hotel. Just walking around outside after day 1 of Minecon was exhilarating, seeing so many people with Minecraft shirts, wearing their official convention bags and merchandise. I was beyond excited. Next I called my buddy Lurgen – his internet handle – with whom I was sharing a room, and he met me at the bar downstairs. Everything was good now. I was with a Diamond Society member live and in person, and we clicked instantly, just like we did online. I had worried it might be awkward to hang out with someone you'd previously only known online, but it was no problem at all. It was amazing.

Later that night I called Jenn to check on her. It was close to midnight for me, so it was almost 2 a.m. in Texas. When I reached her, she was *just* leaving the band. She and the girls had spent nearly twelve hours with Twelve Foot Ninja. I was so happy for her. She told me, albeit quickly, about her day, how she got to watch the Ninja Huddle backstage before the show, and stood on stage in the wing and see the show from there. She told me something even more incredible. Kin and Stevic said to her that *Invincible* and *Sick* from their new album were *her* on the album. They had already started writing *Invincible* but hit a wall with it. Once they focused the song around Jenn, the rest came, and it ended up being one of, if not their biggest single at that point. Jenn also said that when they were performing it on stage, Kin looked back at her with tears in his eyes. It was one of the several times the band members glanced at her, as if to to check on her and make sure she was okay. What an incredible group of guys they are.

They spent more time together after the set ended early due to rain. She said she still loved it, and that they got to perform all of her favorites before it was over. They spent the rest of the day hanging out. Band members would come and go, watching other bands perform. Jenn shared one on one, meaningful conversations with each band member. I felt incredibly happy for her. I have never wanted so badly to be in two places at once. I apologized again that I wasn't there to share all of that with her, but Jenn reassured me that I was right where she wanted me. She was excited to hear that I'd met up with Lurgen, that we connected just like we always had online, and that she was excited for me to meet some of the other Diamond Society members the next day and hoped that I would enjoy the convention. And at that point, she was thoroughly exhausted. We said our good nights.

I won't go into too much detail about Minecon. It was great to meet up with several of my friends from the server. One of the guys goes by BC. We stuck together the entire day and savored hanging out in person. BC took over the duties of running the group when I became too distracted and time-constrained to do a proper job. We went to the same panels, checked out the exhibit hall together, attended meet ups with famous Minecrafters and all of that good stuff.

At Minecon 2016.

BC had arranged for me to have a one on one encounter with my all-time favorite Minecraft YouTuber, GoodTimesWithScar. BC had told him my story after a panel and said he knew it would greatly lift me up if I could meet him, so they set up a date. Scar has a disease that is slowly weakening his body over time. He hasn't been able to walk for several years, but still finds ways to live and love life. He hasn't just been an inspiration to me as a Minecraft builder, but he's an inspiration as a person, too.

By far my favorite parts of the convention were hanging out with the Diamond Society. We ate breakfast together that morning at a Denny's, and then had dinner at a Cheesecake Factory. I also met their family members, which was wonderful.

I decided to miss work on Monday so I wouldn't have to show up after driving through the night. Instead, Lurgen and I went to the airport together Monday morning. My flight was delayed, so we were hanging out for quite a while until his plane left. It was about a six hour drive after landing in Dallas, and I arrived home well after everyone was asleep. I was still exhausted the next day at work, but it was worth it. That was, by far, the most epic weekend of my life.

Bucket List item number six – check.

Unfortunately, Jenn didn't get to do everything she wanted. Despite hundreds of letters to The Ellen Show, Jenn never got an invite. They had her fill out a form for having been nominated, but we never heard back after that.

Shortly after the Twelve Foot Ninja concert, Jenn regressed. Getting out of bed was painful, and she was sleeping more and more. Stephanie offered to buy tickets for them to see Sia, one of Jenn's favorite musical artists, in concert. It was something Jenn had dreamed of doing before she died, but she declined. She was too tired and knew she couldn't make that trip. She also would have liked to see Adele in concert. At one point, when she was still well enough to go, one of her friends had tickets, but something happened and the concert was canceled.

On the upside, the Epic Weekend was helpful to me in many ways. Reflecting on the weekend and life in general on the way home, I realized I had learned a lot from the bucket list journey. Most importantly, you shouldn't wait to do what you want to. I had always believed that, but even so, it is so easy to put things off. We do it out of a sense of responsibility. There's a line in a Dave Matthews song, "The future is no place to place your better days." You have to plan for the future, but at the same time you should take every opportunity you can, to go out and do amazing things.

I pondered, "What can I do to make every day an epic day?" It's probably different for each day. Maybe it means planning my classes better to get more breakthroughs, or to make musical moments happen. It could also be doing something meaningful with the boys – and Jenn at the time – at home.

"What can I do to have an epic month? An epic year? An epic life?" For me, it was being open to possibilities and seizing opportunities when they arise. That was a big idea for me. It helped me find happiness much sooner than anybody expected, and inspired me to share details of my life on Coffee With Coop, and accomplish other goals, like writing this book. I hope it will serve as a constant reminder to do fun things when they pop up, such as going to concerts, traveling, and to try to relax and enjoy life. And yes, you can responsibly plan for the future at the same time. There has to be a balance.

In my opinion, you only get one life, and I'm not convinced anything is waiting for us on the other side. Assuming that's the case, it's imperative we learn how to live it to the fullest. So, let's go. Let's go live an epic life.

Chapter 9

End of Life

"When you die, it does not mean that you lose to cancer. You beat cancer by how you live, why you live, and the manner in which you live."

— STUART SCOTT

EVENTUALLY, TREATMENT ENDS. For the fortunate, it ends with remission. For the rest, it ends in death. Ready or not, the ultimate demise is inescapable. What is life like during this time? There will be good moments, but unless you're lucky enough to live in a place with Death With Dignity laws, it's probably going to be an extremely depressing, drawn-out and paralyzing period. Jenn's end of life was the most difficult, upsetting, heartbreaking, gut-wrenching ordeal I have ever had to endure.

You get here in one of two ways. Either the doctor determines that treatment is doing more harm than good, and recommends discontinuation. Or your loved one develops so much anxiety about going through any more medical procedures that they themselves decide they are done.

I want to share my thoughts on the latter. When the patient elects to stop treatment, don't argue or put up a fight. Tell them it's okay, and support whatever choice they make.

I know it's tough, but these decisions do *not* come easily. Patients arrive at this place after fighting the disease for many months or years. Therapies often inflict terrible side effects, many worse than the disease itself. It's probably a different situation if the diagnosis is not terminal. I highly doubt I would have let Jenn quit when she was at stage 2B, for instance. At that point you still have a shot at beating this thing.

Let's be real, once the cancer metastasizes or a terminal prognosis is given, death is inevitable. Consider the delicate balance, the quantity versus the quality of life. Sometimes treatment can be used to regulate the pain caused by the illness. But there will come a point when continuing to treat the untreatable becomes a waste of precious time.

Jenn stuck with it until her doctor told her, "You can keep undergoing treatment if you want to, but I don't recommend it." The drugs had done so much damage to her body that her spleen and other organs were heavily impacted. "Eventually, your spleen will burst. Soon after that, you'll go into kidney failure, and then your organs will start to shut down one by one." Jenn had already been contemplating stopping treatment for a while by then, so the conclusion was obvious. "Try to enjoy the rest of the time you have left," was her doctor's final advice.

There had been several previous instances when she had considered ending treatment, and I always told her I would stand behind her, no matter what. Why? I wanted her to suffer as little as possible. Trust me, there will come a time when the patient's quality of life is so low, you wish for them to die.

I tried to be as supportive as possible. Jenn needed to know I had her back, always. It was her body, her cancer, her life, her death, her rules, her way. I was just along for the ride and to help out in any way I could.

Starting hospice care elicited several deep emotions. It was depressing to realize that our ability to extend Jenn's life had come to an end. She didn't qualify for any medical trials due to the tumors in her brain. Brain cancer is often considered hopeless, and most experimental studies won't accept a patient with that diagnosis. We looked. There were only two ongoing trials for metastatic breast cancer in Texas at the time, and she was declined for both. Another sad moment in an endless stream of disappointments.

However, we also felt a sense of relief. We had been on the cancer journey for a couple of years by then, more than half of which was merely life-extending therapy. There had been a lot of chemotherapy, a lot of radiation treatments, a lot of medications, a lot of Jenn being emotionally and physically wrecked by various side effects. Just a lot. After all that, we were glad it was over.

We had been looking forward to a brief window of Jenn getting better as the chemotherapy side effects would wear off. She had hoped by starting hospice early, she might be able to enjoy a bit of normalcy before the cancer got entirely out of control. Her fear was starting hospice too late, and not ever feeling good one last time.

Because of the brain tumors, though, that never happened anyway. Jenn had to take steroids to control the brain swelling, which was a side effect of stereotactic radial surgery to her brain, a sort of precision radiation they can do. It left what was essentially a bruise on her brain that caused massive swelling, which could be fatal if not controlled. Due to excessive water retention and an increase in appetite, the steroids caused her to regain all the weight she had worked so hard to lose, and made her feel extremely unwell. Still, we expected she would at least be better than she had been in a long time, once the chemo side effects were gone.

I even went so far as to anticipate Jenn to become completely pain free. A band director mentor of mine had shared this with me, when his mom was in hospice, "They did an incredible job," he said, "She was in no pain, all the way until the very end. She felt no pain. They'll take good care of Jenn." The idea of Jenn being without pain for the first time in over two years sounded great, even if it meant her death was closing in. I just didn't want her to suffer anymore.

So, we experienced a familiar mess of emotions, relief and sadness all at once. Jenn's doctors still had not given us any end-of-life timeframe, and we hoped that meant it would be a long while until then, even knowing her cancer had a ninety-eight percent growth rate. We walked into this new and final chapter together, determined to make the most of whatever time we had left.

Initially, the mood was upbeat. A hospice team from San Angelo came to the house, providing us with an upgraded breathing machine, and an emergency medical kit. Jenn's caseworker happened to be a life-long friend of Cindy's, who had watched Jenn grow up, and her nurse touted having decades of experience.

The nurse seemed a little pushy, but she gave us a good reason for her assertiveness. If Jenn followed her instructions precisely, she would be able to administer excellent pain control. She told us horror stories of patients refusing to comply with her directions, who ended up suffering unnecessarily. Personally, I don't mind when a passionate and experienced professional demands something be done a specific way.

We also got a visit from a chaplain. Perhaps you were hoping I would now offer advice on maintaining your faith under these circumstances. Unfortunately, I can't help with that. I was raised Christian, but gave up those beliefs a little over two years into my marriage with Jenn, after several years of struggling with my faith. Jenn kept hers until the reoccurrence. She had been praying constantly throughout her first round with cancer, and when it returned, she prayed some more. But as she continued getting worse, she developed serious doubts about God. I won't go into the details here, but essentially, Jenn could not reconcile why an almighty God allowed such a tragedy to happen to good people, including innocent children. Her prayers for a cure ultimately remained unanswered. If indeed there is a God, he doomed my wife to being ripped away from her young sons, and condemned our children to a life without their loving mother. We were a happy family, and all her prayers and faith did exactly nothing to prevent her death. Can you blame Jenn for giving up on him?

As a result, she was skeptical about the helpfulness of a chaplain. He turned out to be a friendly guy, who offered to talk about anything Jenn wanted to – no religious topics required, and promised he would not try to convert her. If she was okay with it, he would be happy to just keep her company for a bit. Jenn ended up enjoying his visits, and I still run into him every once in a while.

The emergency medical kit was primarily pain medication. By this time, Jenn was on very strong prescription drugs. The medicine in this pouch was for what is called "breakthrough pain," which is when the pain flares up and gets out of control, despite being heavily medicated already. It would provide fast-acting relief until her regular pain management regimen could take over.

The dream of Jenn ever feeling better or having more energy again was crushed, when we found ourselves in an impossible predicament trying to regulate her pain. She needed high doses of drugs just to not be in total agony. But the amount of medication required for her to actually be pain-free would simply render her unconscious. We decided to violate the nurse's orders, after all. Jenn felt that if she couldn't spend at least some time with us every day, then what was the point? So, she chose to be in considerable discomfort, but awake and present, rather than sleeping the rest of her life away.

At times this balancing act became a point of contention between us. I wanted her free from pain, but she wanted to live. I was afraid of what might happen if she strayed too far from her drug regimen.

The day of the Twelve Foot Ninja concert, Jenn decided she was only going to take Ibuprofen. I can't remember all the medications she was taking then, but I knew it meant she was skipping the heavy painkillers. She insisted she did not want to sleep away any part of that day. I had seen her almost go into shock and feel like she was dying from too much pain before, so I thought it was a terrible idea.

Jenn was furious with me for fighting her on the issue. She had been looking forward to that day for over a year. The possibility of her sleeping through any of it, the way she had missed most of the second Bayside concert, was not up for discussion. She was so livid with me, I had to leave the hotel room.

I went down to the lobby to get some coffee and calm down. When Becky walked in, she saw me sitting there, and came over to check in. I told her about the drama, then we both went upstairs. In the end Jenn got her will. During the drive to the concert she slowly got over our argument. By the time we arrived, excitement had replaced her frustration with me. But it had not been a good start to the day. Fortunately, Jenn had an incredible day, likely fueled by adrenaline. She did pay a heavy price the next day when she was in extreme pain during the car ride home, and required several days to recover and get her pain back to normal levels. Jenn was determined to live in agony rather than sleep until her death.

Jenn's disposition and quality of life further deteriorated. The fight against the pain was constant. She waited until it got excruciating before resorting to the potent drugs. When she took those regularly, she was only awake for a few hours each day.

Jenn being asleep so much was depressing for myself and the boys. It had been nice having her around more at the beginning of hospice, when she was up and alert longer than she had been in the months prior. She tried to time her few waking hours to be in the evening, so they would line up with the last hour before the boys went to bed. This way she could be part of their nighttime routine, yet still talk to me and be on the computer to check on social media or catch up with her favorite YouTubers.

The sense of death looming closely, yet having to waste much of her precious time sleeping, caused Jenn's mood to reach new lows. She did always put on a brave face for the boys. But many days she was understandably frustrated and bitter. For me, it was disheartening. This was not what we had imagined hospice being like, not how we had wanted the end of her life to play out. There was zero comfort for any of us.

The boys and I felt her impending death. Almost every night, one of the boys, if not both, would ask me, "Dad, when is mom going to die?"

"I just don't know, buddy." I would say, my heart breaking each time. "But I promise, when mom dies, we're going to be okay." By now I understood it was my job to reassure them, to give them hope. "One day, we'll even be happy again."

Devin and Kayden asked me all kinds of questions about the future. Jenn had already told them I might get married again one day, and that they would have a stepmom then. She wanted them to give someone a real chance at being their mom, but also to let me know if that woman was mean to them behind my back.

Naturally the boys were curious about that. "When are you going to get married again?" they asked. "What is your next wife going to look like?" Kayden wondered.

"Guys, I have no idea. I'm not even thinking about that right now. It will probably be a long time. We're going to live life with just the three of us for a long time."

Then I realized that prospect might seem a bit depressing, so I tried to make it sound good somehow. For example, I promised Devin we would be able to have his friends spend the night at our house again. I said to both they wouldn't have to be super quiet at home anymore. They would be allowed to turn the TV up louder when playing games, and could run around and play like they used to. I had to give them something, so the future didn't seem bleak. Judge me if you must, but looking for these silver linings was a helpful tool.

Jenn and I were soulmates, but also opposites. She was a consumerist, while I wanted to pay off our debts and start saving money so we could retire rich. I preferred an organized house, but she was too attached to possessions to let them go, exhibiting almost hoarder-like tendencies, which made it impossible to maintain a clean and orderly house. Not that I was the virtuous one in all our opposing traits. She had a great sense of humor, whereas mine has been pretty flat, or at best, dry. I have rarely, if ever, been intentionally funny. She was hilarious. My parenting style didn't always take the boys' emotions into account, while Jenn could read them like a book, making her better at giving concise lectures and dealing out fair punishments. We complemented each other very well. But still, the house and our finances bothered me. I had to learn to accept and forget these issues, focusing on everything good in our life instead.

A year of therapy, antidepressants, and self-reflection had changed my perspective. After having operated in single dad mode for so long, I was now able to imagine a life without Jenn that might not be all bad.

I made plans to create a monthly budget and overpay on our remaining debts, so I could start saving money for the boys' college, and what I hope will be an awesome retirement. I had tried doing this before, when I was still in college, with just Jenn's income and my student loan refunds. Back then, if we paid all our bills, we each had only ten dollars a week for anything else. Jenn rebelled, and that was the end of that. I didn't bring it up again for the rest of our marriage.

An early attempt at keeping a neat house suffered the same fate. After reading Organizing for Dummies, I followed the book's outlines, creating a super efficient and tidy apartment. I didn't get to the bedrooms, but I had completed the hallway, hallway closet, living room, and kitchen. When Jenn came home to find everything reorganized, she threw a fit, and told me to never mess with her kitchen again. I was looking forward to finally bringing some order to our chaotic house.

I even began considering I might fall in love again someday, though it was hard to imagine how exactly that was going to happen. My life was so busy, I had no time for a relationship. I wasn't interested in anyone at work, and didn't go anywhere else. There were the band director conventions, but strangely enough, I don't think I would be compatible with a female band director. Most of them, men and women, have large egos, and that's not me.

At least, thanks primarily to Jenn, I was open to the idea of dating, if not optimistic about my chance of actually meeting someone. Just contemplating it was a huge step. After all, I was already pretty lonely. I still had Jenn, but she was asleep most of the time. We maybe spent thirty minutes to an hour together, not quite every night, and that time, while precious to me, didn't feel the same as it used to.

More than anything, I was looking forward to Jenn not suffering anymore. She didn't allow herself to be knocked out completely, so whenever she was awake, she was in excruciating pain, and it would continue to be this way for the rest of her short life. The idea of her death devastated me, but the idea of her spending whatever time she had left in such agony broke my heart. There was no good outcome.

Despite feeling my life would get easier or even better once Jenn was gone, I never wished for her death to come more quickly. At least not until the very end. I always wanted her to live as long and as fully as she could. But for the first time in years, I had hope. I had hope we would be okay one day, even happy. I had to be confident, for my sake, but especially for the boys. It was going to be up to me to make sure we could be happy again, even without Jenn.

"At what point do I need to take off work?" I asked both the hospice nurse and caseworker. They informed me of a law allowing family members in situations such as ours to take off work for a certain prolonged period of time without losing their job. I should request the paperwork from my school district now, so it would be ready to go. If they didn't have the proper forms, the caseworker would provide me with a general application from the state.

The nurse said it would be best to stay home approximately two or three weeks before the end, and that she would let me know when the time came. I was reassured for the moment, though in reality she will only visit every so often. Maybe it's different if you live in a city, but our closest hospice location was over an hour away. Initially, the nurse came by once a week. As Jenn's condition deteriorated, someone checked in every few days, more often only in case of emergency. Ultimately, it was up to me alone to figure out when Jenn needed me full time.

One day she called me while I was in class. An emergency. I had no details, just that Jenn needed me home right away. The secretary found someone to cover for me, and I rushed to get there as fast as I could.

I entered the house to find Jenn walking around fully dressed, and visibly upset. "Jenn, what's going on?" I said, confused.

"Help me, Chris! We were supposed to be on the road already, and we're not even packed!" she exclaimed.

"We're not going anywhere, babe. What are you talking about?"

"The concert! We're supposed to go to the concert, and if we don't leave soon we're going to miss it! I've been waiting to go to this concert for a long time! How did you not know about this? We've had this planned for a long time! And we should already be packed, now help me!"

I was perplexed. In my bewilderment, I wasn't able to think clearly enough to consider that something might be wrong with Jenn's brain, or that she could be experiencing side effects from a medication. I had no idea what exactly was going on, but she was obviously severely confused and distressed.

"Jenn, we don't have any more concerts to go to, remember? We already went to all of our concerts." I started to explain.

"No, we have a concert to go to," she replied with absolute certainty, "and you're not helping me pack! Now help me!"

"Babe, who are we going to see? Where is the concert?"

She looked at me, appalled, in silence. Then she said, "I... I can't remember. My memory must be cloudy from my meds or something. But I *know* we have a concert to go to!"

"We already went to all of our concerts, babe. Remember? We went to see Bayside with Becky in San Antonio? And the last one we went to was to meet Twelve Foot Ninja in Dallas? That was our last one, babe. We don't have any more concerts to go to. I'm sorry, but we don't have any more concerts to go to." I was really worried at this point, wishing Jenn would have a moment of clarity so I could get through to her.

Jenn was silent for a second. I thought she was starting to figure it out, but then she shouted, "How do you not remember? You don't believe me? Fine, I'll call Becky! She'll tell you!" She grabbed her phone and pulled up Becky's contact info, dialing the number, "I can't believe you don't believe me! How can you not remember?" Instead of getting more lucid, she was doubling down, trying to prove she was right. I didn't know it at the time, but this was only the first instance of what would become a terrible behavior pattern.

Becky answered. Jenn explained how I wasn't helping her get ready for the concert, that we were going to miss it, and could she please tell me that we were going to this concert. Becky was just as confused as I was, and took the same approach, trying to gently point out that there was no concert. Perhaps she was thinking of the Twelve Foot Ninja concert, but we had already attended that one.

Jenn listened to Becky. Perhaps she had just needed a second opinion to convince her. She sat down on the bed, still confused, but possibly coming to her senses. It was hard to tell for sure. "I really thought we had a concert to go to," she said in a sad voice.

"I really wish we did, babe." I was weighed down by the crushing reality that there truly weren't any more concerts left. "Maybe you were having a flashback?"

"Maybe..." she said, her mind drifting off.

"Do you want to lay down and rest for a bit?" I asked. She accepted, and before long she was asleep. I sat in my computer chair, mentally and emotionally spent. Did she have a flashback? What *was* that? Was this an isolated incident, or would it happen again?

I called Adrian later that evening to vent about it. I told him it might be time for me to take off work. He understood that meant I would be out for weeks, or until her death. Adrian promised he would cover my classes, and not to worry about work.

Jenn woke up that evening, behaving completely normally. She remembered being confused earlier in the day, but neither one of us could figure out why. Perhaps it was denial, or some level of naiveté that led me to believe she would be fine, that she was back to her old self, that it had been a solitary event. So the next morning I went to work as usual.

That evening, the nurse came by. During each visit she counted Jenn's medication, to confirm she had enough and was taking it as prescribed. Everything had always been fine, but this time she made a surprising discovery.

Jenn was over-medicating. It came as a complete shock to me. For the entirety of our cancer journey, she had been very organized, diligent, and prompt about taking her medicine. The scary part was that she hadn't been doing it on purpose. She was drifting in and out of consciousness so much, she didn't always check to make sure it was the right time for the next round of meds. She only knew she was waking up in pain.

It was not Jenn's fault, though. Ideally, whenever she was hurting too much before the next dose was due, I should have given her the breakthrough morphine included in the emergency pouch. Then, based on how often I had to do that, the medical team could have adjusted her prescription accordingly.

The fact remained that Jenn had been unknowingly overdosing on morphine pills. It is possible for opiates to induce hallucinations, which could very well have been the reason for the episode the previous day. That was it for me.

"Fuck that," I said to myself, and later to Adrian, "Work isn't that important." It was painfully obvious that Jenn could no longer care for herself while I was at work. She needed someone present full-time, if only to be in charge of the medication for now. It was clearly my responsibility. I sent an e-mail to my administrators and entered the remainder of my personal days into the time-off request system. This was it. The end was near.

Jenn and I were fortunate she had a dedicated mother and friends, who cared enough to show up when we needed them. If friends and family don't volunteer their support, it is worth it to directly ask them for as much help as you can get. Once Jenn was stuck in bed and required assistance just to sit up, taking care of her wasn't an easy task. She didn't need constant attention since she slept most of the time, but it was an extremely difficult job, especially during her waking hours.

Cindy had been begging to come live with us for months, ever since Jenn started hospice care. She yearned to take care of her baby, despite her own handicap after two major strokes. Not being able to be with Jenn tore her apart.

Jenn, however, did not want her mom at the house. She felt that Cindy staying with us meant the end was near. She wasn't emotionally ready for it, despite deeply loving her mom.

Every couple of weeks Cindy brought up the subject to me, sometimes in tears. Eventually even Charles, Jenn's step-dad, spoke up, urging me to let Cindy move in. But Jenn was still able to go to the restroom on her own, and to the kitchen to get food. And most importantly, she wasn't ready yet, so regardless of what Cindy or Charles wanted, I was going to enforce Jenn's wishes.

Nevertheless, after the recent episodes of confusion and over-medication, Becky and I decided it was time for Cindy to stay with us. Jenn protested. She did not want to admit how close, perhaps only a few weeks away, her death was. In the end we were able to convince her. Jenn did request we tell her mom not to spend every waking moment in the room with her, so she could have some privacy. That seemed reasonable enough.

Becky had traveled down after the disturbing phone call about the concert. Clearly Jenn needed her now. Becky ended up going back and forth between work and our house until the final two or three weeks, during which she was with us for all but a few days.

Jenn was like a sister to Becky. She had taken time off work in the past to help care for her. Becky's employers were aware of the situation, and allowed her to be absent for extended periods as Jenn's death became imminent. Because she didn't get paid for the missed time like I did, the financial strain was significant, so Cindy and I helped with her bills that month. For Jenn to have her best friend be there was more than worth it.

Several other friends came by to see Jenn one last time, but ended up staying for the day to help out. Some of them even made two or three trips. One of Jenn's close friends, Stephanie, spent several days at the house with us. Kisha, a stage IV cancer sister, who had previously flown in to visit in person, managed to scrape together enough money to come out and stay for a couple of weeks. It was the best hospice team you could possibly ask for.

It did get a little crowded, but I was so grateful to have the help. Initially there was some confusion about whether or not Jenn had been given her medication at any given time, but we quickly fixed that by keeping a logbook. None of us slept for long periods anyway, so for the most part we were able to handle these logistics by simply talking to each other, but we had the log, just in case.

Having the women in the house made taking care of Jenn a lot easier for me. They ended up doing most of the work. I gave Jenn the bulk of her medication, which I detested, but the ladies helped her to the restroom. Jenn had insisted on that. She dreaded the day I would have to wipe her, so she recruited Becky, Stephanie, and her mom early on, specifically for that task. Each time I volunteered to take her to the bathroom, even when she could barely talk, and wasn't able to refuse me herself anymore, the ladies didn't allow it. They were enforcing her wishes until the end.

I couldn't stand giving Jenn medication. After the overdosing incident, we had to get very strict with her drug regimen. We ended up having to use a lot more of the breakthrough medicine, until the medical team figured out how to manage her pain by adjusting the regular dosage. The emergency kit consisted of opiates in patches and liquid form. The transdermal patches were no big deal, but Jenn loathed the taste of the liquid morphine. Giving her Dr. Pepper or Pepsi to chase it down with didn't improve the flavor.

The main reason all of us, including Jenn, hated the drugs so much, was they meant Jenn was going to go back to sleep. Or worse, stay asleep. She was awake less than three hours a day. Pushing liquid medicine into her mouth while she slept made me feel incredibly guilty. I was depriving her of the ability to wake up and live. It was necessary though, and I was well aware of that. It became blatantly obvious the closer we got to the end, because we never knew which Jenn we could expect when she woke up.

At first, Jenn was her normal self. By normal, I mean mostly depressed and tired. Still, she tried to enjoy chatting with the ladies and me. All of us were looking forward to those moments, treasuring them. We never knew when a conversation with Jenn might be our last.

Less than one week after her first bout of confusion, Jenn woke up one night, and suddenly...

"Chris... Oh my God, Chris, look!"

"What is it?" I asked.

"Look, on the wall over there! You don't see that?" Jenn was more than concerned; she was appalled.

"There are bugs all over the wall! Look!"

I did. There was nothing. Jenn was clearly delusional again, but this was different. She was hallucinating. It was an instant blow to my psyche, because I had read online that hallucinations were a sign death might be merely days away. But in those articles they were describing people seeing loved ones who had passed away, which I wouldn't have minded so much.

"Babe, listen to me," I said calmly. She looked at me with wide eyes and her mouth agape. I wasn't sure what to do, but I didn't want her to be in constant fear and discomfort thinking our house had an infestation, so I stated, "I know you see bugs on the wall over there, but they're not real. They can't hurt you because they're not really there. You don't have to be afraid of them."

Jenn looked perplexed. She had her thinking face on. "You don't see them?"

"No, babe, I don't see them. I know you see them, but they're not really there. It's just a hallucination. But everything is okay. There aren't any bugs in the house, so you don't have to be afraid. Try not to worry about it."

Jenn wasn't having it. She got out of bed and went to the wall to examine the imaginary insects up close. "No, they're right here! Ugh, they're disgusting! What kind of bugs are they?"

"Jenn, please, get back in bed. They're not real, and they can't hurt you."

She stood defiantly, and motioned with her hand toward the wall. "What, are you saying I'm going crazy? Chris, I *see* the bugs. They're *right there*, all over the wall! Can you please *do* something about them?"

I didn't want to give up. In my heart I believed I could get Jenn to understand what was happening. I was convinced it was the only way she would feel safe. If she could comprehend that what she was seeing wasn't real, maybe she would be able to detach herself, and not be so afraid. I didn't want her living in constant fear, especially if these delusions were going to get worse. So, I kept trying to explain it to her. As a result Jenn got upset, because I wasn't taking care of the bugs, but went to get Becky.

When Becky came in and confirmed what I had said, Jenn listened, stunned. I could tell she was deeply distressed and disheartened about what had happened, but she finally trusted us, and went back to bed. A few moments later, she asked if we could wipe down the wall, just to make her feel better, and we obliged. When we did so, the bugs went away. We spent the rest of the night with Jenn, who was trying to understand how she could have possibly been imagining the bugs. They seemed so real, she said. She couldn't identify them. They weren't ants, and she wasn't able to find pictures online. They were some kind of exotic, color-changing insect, unlike any of us had ever seen. When she woke up, she was fine.

Jenn was hallucinating a lot after this incident. Once or twice it was mice, but mostly bugs. The infestations grew more extreme over time, from one wall to the entire house. She had bursts of energy and started cleaning like crazy, yelling at bystanders if they weren't helping.

Early on, Becky and I were able to convince her she was hallucinating. But when friends played along with the delusions, cleaning walls for her immediately, Jenn felt betrayed. She gave me a death stare, exclaiming, "You see! They see it! I knew I wasn't going crazy! Why would you tell me I was hallucinating?" her voice cracked as she said the last part. Becky and I were furious. Once someone other than Becky, her mom and I had verified the bugs were real, she was unyielding. Worse, she no longer trusted me.

Faced with this impossible predicament, Cindy also told Jenn the bugs were real, claiming she had only said they weren't, because she didn't want her to be scared. It was probably a smart decision. Jenn still felt deceived by her mom, too, but was willing to accept the justification. Her friends explained to us they had previously seen similar symptoms with dying loved ones, and that in their experience it was best to go along with it, and follow whatever requests they may have. I could not understand why you would *want* to let Jenn think the infestation was real. To this day, I still have doubts about the way I handled it. Was I right? Were they right? What is the best way to comfort someone going through that? I wish I knew.

Dealing with it was a perpetual battle. Jenn would get out of bed and clean like mad. One time she got hold of insect repellent, excessively spraying it all over the house to the point of toxicity. We wrestled the spray can away from her, hid it where she wouldn't find it again, and aired out the house, but it was scary to imagine what other lengths she might go to in her efforts to get rid of the imaginary infestation.

There were other trying situations. Close to the end, Jenn didn't remember who any of us were. For me, that was quite difficult.

Her friends tried to make it fun for her. For example, one of them once said, "Hey, there's this really cute guy sitting over there, and he's checking you out!" Jenn gave me an intense look, like she was both flattered and interested. It was a cute and thoughtful attempt to help her reconnect with me. A few minutes later she remembered who I was, except for some reason she was now convinced I was cheating on her. She became furious with me, and I had to leave the room so she could calm down. I went to the living room and cried. I understood it wasn't her fault, but it still cut me deeply. No amount of understanding helped with that.

Jenn hated her condition so much that on several occasions she begged us to kill her. Well, she asked her friends and her mom, not me. Cindy calmly explained that she couldn't do that, because if she went to prison, she wouldn't be able to help me or the boys. Jenn didn't care. "Well, you just have to buck up and do it, anyway. Please, Mom, I need you to do this! You have to!" Episodes like these were devastating to all of us, though not surprising. She was in an intense amount of pain, and lived in a permanent state of fear and panic due to the confusion and hallucinations. Early on she had always joked that if things ever got this bad, to just kill her. Unfortunately, there was absolutely nothing we could legally do, besides give her more pain medication and watch her die slowly and in agony.

There were good times, too, periods where Jenn was completely lucid. We enjoyed those a lot, joking around, having normal conversations.

I got to hug and kiss her, each moment like that becoming more precious and bittersweet, as she was hallucinating more frequently.

We did what we could to take care of ourselves. I spent most of my time at the computer desk, which was wedged right up to my side of the bed, so I could keep a close eye on Jenn at all times. One of the ladies occasionally took my place, so I could sit in the living room.

Becky and I went on a few walks, to talk about what was going on. My anger issues returned during this period, and I vented to Becky. Part of me felt guilty about what I had to say. In particular, I harbored resentment toward Jenn, because she had regrets about how she had lived with cancer. Things I had tried to talk to her about, such as maintaining a healthy diet for example, but she wouldn't listen, and now she was full of regrets. It got to me. Becky didn't judge me for any of it. She understood I was just processing my emotions. We also talked about how to handle Jenn, Becky's work or family, whatever came to mind to fill the silence.

I delved more heavily than ever into Minecraft. If I was sitting next to the bed, Jenn asleep, I was gaming or watching videos. My emotional state was so dismantled, I did whatever I could to not be in the present moment. In retrospect, that was probably smart. Even so, I was a total mess. The end of Jenn's life was easily, hands down, no contest, the most traumatic period in my life, and there were many times when I was barely hanging on to my sanity.

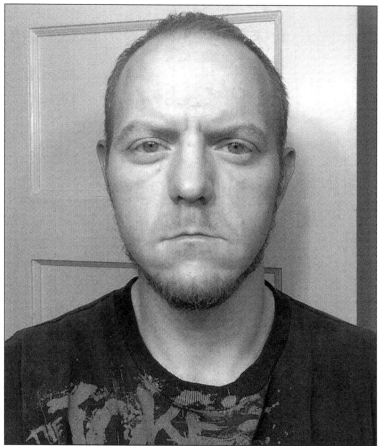

This is the only picture we posted to social media while Jenn was confronting her final days.

The hospice doctor and nurses could not get Jenn's pain under control, even though we followed their instructions precisely. We reported her poor condition over the phone, and they advised us to increase her dosage, which we did, but then there wasn't enough medicine to last until their next visit. When they finally came by, they had failed to adjust the prescription, and only brought the amount of medication she took when her doses had been lower.

We kept explaining that we needed more meds sooner, but they didn't listen. This was a far cry from the supposed to be comforting hospice experience I had read and heard about from friends. It was infuriating. They gave us the impression they couldn't do much about it.

At one point we were completely out of morphine and Jenn was writhing in pain. It was a Saturday, their pharmacy was closed until Monday, and, depending on the order, it would be Monday evening or Tuesday before they could restock our supply. Waiting until Monday was not an option. I was livid. If their pharmacy was closed, they should have been willing to go to a 24-hour pharmacy to fill the prescriptions, but they wouldn't do that.

I decided to take her to the ER. This was in the middle of the night. I called the hospital first, to explain the situation and make sure they could handle it, given their history of permanently disabling Cindy. They said they could get Jenn's pain under control, and to bring her in if we deemed it necessary.

We did. It was well after midnight, and an ambulance ride would cost hundreds of dollars, even if it were just down the street. We worried it would be too painful for Jenn to get in and out of the car, so we put her in the wheelchair and walked several blocks down the street to the local hospital.

Luckily, the nurse practitioner on call was good. Not only did she hook up Jenn with enough pain medication to make her comfortable, but she called hospice on our behalf and forcefully told them off for not listening to us and not meeting Jenn's medical needs. It – was – awesome. Thanks to her, a hospice nurse came by the next morning with enough medication to get us through the day, including a promise that someone would be there the following day with a supply to last until the next regularly scheduled visit. This meant calling in the pharmacist on their day off to prepare the medicine, and mobilizing a nurse on their day off to deliver it to us. In other words, thanks to the nurse practitioner at the local hospital, our hospice team got off their butts to help us during their spare time. It was a problem of their own making, because they had not provided us with any extra medication, in case Jenn's dosage had to go up.

It was stressful, and I hated seeing Jenn in so much pain. After this event, we finally got her to a comfortable place, where she stayed until the end of her life.

During this time, I was incessantly rereading the signs of imminent death and reassessing where we were. You can easily find this list through a Google search, I don't care to go into it here. However, some precursors are that a patient is almost never awake anymore, will stop eating and drinking as the organs shut down, and eventually lose the ability to talk. First Jenn's speech became inarticulate mumbles, then even those were barely audible. It was like communicating with a baby. You could decipher her emotions, but not the words. Once she couldn't speak at all, figuring out what she wanted was an almost impossible challenge.

Jenn was fighting to sit up, but lacked the strength, so we helped put her in a seated position. It turned out being too painful due to the lesions on her diaphragm, so she had to heavily bend over. She was still able to talk a little bit then, and asked Becky to take a picture of the two of us.

From the time she was diagnosed with the reoccurrence, Jenn was keenly aware she needed to take as many pictures with the boys and me as possible. She had spent most of our life together staying out of photos, because she had been so self-conscious about her looks. Now that she was dying, it was one of her many regrets.

I thought about that as Becky held up my phone. I took Jenn's hand and leaned over in my chair to be closer to her. I still have the picture, but it's one I'll never share. Jenn didn't want anyone to see her like that. The moment will stay with me forever though. She wanted one more piece of evidence, one more image, for me to be able to look back on and remember us.

In this phase, Jenn had a brief waking period where she was lucid. I could tell she was clearheaded by her eyes. She looked at me with deep love, but also with deep sorrow. Once again she wanted to sit, but whenever we tried to move her upward, the pain was so intense she could never get there. Therefore, no matter how much she grunted in anger, we refused her requests to help her sit up and reminded her of how much it hurt. Poor Jenn. She was fighting death with every fiber of her being.

She gazed at me with sad, loving eyes, and started to lift her arms. I recognized this as her wanting to hug me. She probably wondered if it was the last hug she could give me. I bent over, putting my arms around her as best I could. Jenn managed to get her arms bent behind my shoulders. She mumbled to me. I simply responded, "I love you, too." I held her, tears streaming down my face, until she finally put her arms down, and then kissed her. "I love you, too, Jenn."

That event was devastatingly tough to get through, but such a meaningful connection with my wife. I have been replaying the moment in my head over and over many times since that day, along with the one below.

After she couldn't vocalize at all anymore, Jenn had another flash of lucidity. As before, I could tell by the expression in her eyes. She looked at me and started to lift her arms for a hug. Except this time, she just didn't have the strength, lifting her hands two inches at the most. Seeing that crushed me, but I quickly went over and gently put my arms around her. In a shaking voice, I told her, "I know, Jenn. I love you, too."

As I recall and write down these final interactions with Jenn – the one above truly being the last one, she only slept after that, I am crying convulsively, but treasuring the memories nonetheless. Somehow, Jenn was able to fight through the hallucinations and the fog of perpetual confusion to let me know, just a few more times, that she loved me. That will always mean the entire world to me.

At some point we knew death was close. By then we had been actively hoping Jenn would go. She was suffering so much. The hallucinations and delusions, the extreme pain, the humiliation of needing the assistance of friends to use the toilet – which eventually was just a portable toilet seat we'd put next to the bed and manually cleaned afterward, her deteriorating ability to communicate with us, and her further degradation to an almost infant-like state, must have been hell on her. It was hell on us, so we could only fathom the fear and pain she must have been enduring.

We loved Jenn. We didn't want to lose her, and yet, in so many ways she was already lost. I think her body and perhaps her gut-level survival instincts were fighting to live well beyond what Jenn had ever reasonably hoped for. She never wanted it to get this bad, and neither did we. So yes, every day for nearly two weeks we hoped she would be ready and just go. We hoped it would be in her sleep, that it would be painless, but we hoped it would be sooner rather than later. Because if there is one devastating truth we all came to realize, it was that the longer she lived, the worse it was going to get, and there seemed to be no bottom to how bad things could get.

We knew it was getting closer and closer, but Jenn clung to life. It could be any hour, any moment, and yet another day would go by. I continued to reassess our situation based on the signs of imminent death I had found online. The problem is, the lists, besides varying to some degree, all state that a person will experience some, but likely not all of the symptoms. Even armed with such information, I was clueless. So I sat at Jenn's side, trying to keep myself preoccupied, and waited for the end.

One night I was convinced it was about to happen. I had promised Jenn I would hold her when she went. I had struggled with the idea for a long time, knowing how traumatic it would be for me. But by now I was hardened, ready to honor my promise, just as I had tried to at Disneyland. Jenn had what many refer to as a death rattle, which had been going on for a day or two at least. The intervals in between each breath had increased, but only slightly. Of everything on the lists, this was perhaps my best indicator. So, I waited, carefully keeping track of her respiration, and looking for some sign that she was at the end.

I waited all through that night, and through the entire next morning, adamant not to miss it. Becky and Cindy tried to tag me out, encouraging me to at least take a nap, but I refused. Of course, you can only go so long without sleep, and by then I was well over the twenty-four hour mark.

I finally hit my limit around lunchtime on December first, 2016. My determination was overpowered by sleep deprivation, so I came up with a plan B. I crawled into bed next to Jenn, draping my right arm over her. I told her I loved her, that this was the best I could do, and that I hoped it was good enough. I also reassured her, for the umpteenth time, that if she was ready to go, it was okay for her to go, that we would be okay. And then I told her one last time that I loved her.

Cindy and Becky were in the room when I laid down. They asked if they should leave the room, but I insisted they could stay. I was so exhausted, I didn't think it would matter. The hospice team had advised us to hang around Jenn even after she couldn't respond anymore, because it would help her feel like she was still part of the group and provide some comfort. That's exactly what they were doing.

Stephanie was also present. She needed to go home that day, but she had volunteered to pick up Taco Bell for Cindy and Becky beforehand. When she got back, Cindy and Becky went to the living room to eat lunch. I was asleep. It was during this ten or fifteen minute window, before Becky returned to the room, when it was just Jenn and I, that she finally passed on.

Jennifer Cooper died on December first, 2016, just after lunchtime, approximately three weeks after her first episode of confusion that caused me to take off from work. She died in her sleep, in my arms, surrounded by most of her closest friends and family, although she waited for them to leave the room. Except that she would have chosen to die before her condition got so bad, everything else about her death was the way she had wanted it to be. I'm taking some measure of comfort in that.

Becky walked back into the room. She had been afraid of being the one to find Jenn dead, that she would have to break the news to Cindy and me. Her fear became reality that day. She woke me up with a certain vacancy in her voice, "Chris, wake up. I think it's over. I think Jenn is dead." I can't recall her exact words, but I clearly remember the tone of her voice. After I was awake, she went to tell Cindy.

I was surprisingly calm. I had rehearsed this moment in my mind countless times, and I was as ready for it as one can be. I felt a bit sad, but mostly calm.

I looked at Jenn. It was the same vibe as seeing my grandfather in the morgue one year earlier. I touched her head. She was still warm, but significantly less warm than she had been. Sign one, check.

I put my ear over her mouth and listened carefully for any breath sounds. There were none, even after waiting for a minute. Sign two, check.

I put my ear to her chest. I remembered the untold number of times I listened to her heartbeat in the ten years we had been together. It was sadly absent now. Sign three, check.

Becky was right. Jenn was dead.

I sat back up, stared at her face, and just sighed. Part of me was sad that she was now gone forever. Another part of me was relieved that this very long and hellish road was over, that her suffering had ended. There was no joy in this, however, just relief. My thoughts quickly turned to the boys, who were in school. One of us had been picking them up from school every day, with instructions to make sure Jenn was still alive before they came inside. If she wasn't, we wanted that person to try to prepare them for what they were going to see when they looked at her. We had already had these conversations with them, but we really didn't want them to be surprised.

I was alert, but definitely not in a state to drive. We asked one of Jenn's local cancer sisters if she would pick up the boys for us, and try to let them know before they came into the house. She agreed, and I was grateful.

Cindy came into the room with a heavier heart than I ever care to imagine, and hope I never have to experience myself. She was surprisingly well put together, though. Like me, she was sad, but composed, and somewhat relieved to see her daughter's intense suffering come to an end. I think she eventually cried, but not much.

It was so different from how I had imagined Cindy and I would react. Becky was almost always calm in difficult situations, so I wasn't completely surprised – though I still worried about her. And I am typically calm in a crisis, but I had figured this one would be too close to home for that instinct to kick in. It kicked in for all of us. The mood in the house was sullen, but not anguished.

Perhaps an hour later, the boys arrived home. I went to meet them at the door. "Dad, is Mom really dead?" one of them asked.

"Yes, but it's okay. She looks like she's asleep." I said that, because they had all kinds of crazy ideas about what a dead person looked like. With zombies being a culture craze, along with stories of vampires and other undead monsters, there's no telling how many different images they had in their heads, of what their mom would look like when she was dead. These notions kept coming back, even after explaining the reality to them several times over the last year and a half. I reassured them once more. "She looks completely normal, but like she's asleep. She just isn't breathing and doesn't have a heartbeat. Other than that, she looks exactly like you remember. Do you want to see her?"

They both did, so I walked them back to the bedroom. The boys were obviously sad, but they were also surprisingly calm. I suppose we had all been ready for this for a long time.

I had read in a book that children might want to do all kinds of things with their deceased loved ones, and that this should be encouraged. It could include hugging, cuddling, kissing, but also a straightforward medical exam, where they might experiment by lifting up limbs and feeling the skin in different parts of the body. In the boys' case, they just wanted to give their mom a hug and a kiss, and say their goodbyes. It was hard to watch, but I kept myself together for it.

Later Devin asked to play at a friend's house down the street. We sent both boys over, where they played with friends and ate dinner, while we dealt with all the commotion ensuing at our house.

Several formalities had to take place. An officer from the sheriff's department came by to get a visual confirmation. I'm not sure who called to report it, but I remember we needed to dial the non-emergency line. That officer then called a Justice of the Peace, who brought with him the head sheriff and another deputy. One of the deputies supervised Becky as she disposed of Jenn's narcotics.

A hospice nurse eventually arrived and examined Jenn, then pronounced her official time of death, which was about four hours after her actual time of death.

Several friends and family showed up once they heard. Adrian and Donna visited to say their goodbyes. Stephanie turned around and came back.

My dad hurried into town. Like Cindy, he had been anxious to be at my side during this time of crisis, but Jenn didn't want anyone outside her most inner circle seeing her the way she was, so I had to refuse him. Once she was dead, however, I told him it was okay, and he showed up practically running. Charles and Cindy's sister got there shortly after. Between all of the friends, family, and officials, it was a full house.

I didn't mind, though. I divided my time between Jenn's corpse, trying to soak in her face and what was left of her presence before it was too late, and conversing with everyone else who was there.

Eventually, two gentlemen from the funeral home showed up to take her body. You see, you don't call an ambulance in the event of a death, because it's not an emergency. You call the police. Normally they would have the body picked up by the morgue, but in Jenn's case, no autopsy was necessary. Her cause of death was well documented. So the funeral home came to get her.

I watched them bring in a stretcher and carefully position her onto it. If I wasn't already in a daze, seeing this happen in real time certainly put me in one. It was surreal. I felt far away, yet present, as I absorbed every detail I could. They placed a sheet over her body, and that was it. I would never see her face again. I remember walking into the living room, trying to get out of their way, and then watching as they carefully carried her through the house, watching as Jenn passed me by.

This was the moment Cindy finally broke, fully and completely. She cried uncontrollably, begging for Jenn not to go. My heart sank for her. All the same, she did so great that day. Her strength was unbelievable. And fortunately, her husband was there to hold her close.

We continued to look on as they placed her into the back of a van and closed the doors. That was it. We would never see her again.

Chapter 10

Out of Hell

"If you're going through hell, keep going."

– WINSTON CHURCHILL

I WANT TO PREFACE this chapter by saying that, while you can never be fully prepared for the death of a spouse or a parent, the boys and I were as ready as one can be. We had missed very few therapy sessions over the course of the past year. I had been on antidepressants for almost as long. While Jenn was in hospice, I asked my doctor to adjust the medication, because I had been starting to feel severely depressed again, so she added a second drug to my regimen. I had built a great support network, including hundreds of Jenn's followers cheering us on at my Coffee With Coop page, as well as friends I'd had for decades, and family who had been there my entire life. I had built a solid routine, allowing me to coast on autopilot and take care of myself and the boys while processing our new situation. Jenn's slow decline meant I had been gradually transitioning into that new life, slowly taking on more household responsibilities, and spending most of my day without her company. Being relatively young helped. My therapist told me that while ten years is a significant time to be with someone, it's not as long as thirty or fifty years, and that because of my age, I could potentially bounce back more quickly.

Besides losing Jenn, which was extremely unlucky, everything else about our situation seemed quite lucky, indeed. We had as smooth a transition into a new life as one could hope for, especially considering it was a transition none of us had ever wanted to make. I feel worse for people who lose their spouse or co-parent suddenly in an accident, or who discover cancer at such a late stage that they only have weeks or days left. We had two and a half years to prepare.

Not to suggest the process was easy because it was gradual. Just different. Rather than beginning the grieving process when Jenn died, I started when I realized her chances of survival after five years were zero percent. During the first round with cancer I tried to convince my family and myself that she could beat it, that we would be happy again, but a side of me was already freaking out about living without her.

While my grief continued after Jenn's death, I was far along in the process. My hope is that in sharing this, I can encourage caregivers who do have the benefit of advance warning, as I did, to use the extra time to not just get by, but to get ready. Because whether you like it or not, ready or not, death is coming. Allow yourself the space to grieve the loss of your spouse as it happens, piece by piece. By the time you reach the end, there will only be a tiny fragment of them left. We lost Jenn well before her death. When she died, there was very little left of her to lose.

Hospice still sucked. Seeing Jenn suffering was by far the most difficult thing we had to go through in the entire two-and-a-half-year journey. It was so overwhelmingly stressful, that when Jenn died, the sense of losing what little was left of her was overpowered by the relief that she didn't have to suffer anymore.

Everyone's grief journey is unique, but I believe we all go through the same basic process. Some people move more quickly, which is what many think I did, especially if not factoring in the years I spent grieving before Jenn's death, while others take several years. Some try to hang onto their loved ones for as long as possible, and others rip the band-aid off. Most are somewhere in the middle.

I chose to rip the band-aid off. I saw no point in hanging on to anything for longer than I had to. After two and a half years of depression, a year and a half of which I spent living in limbo between my old life and a new life I knew was coming whether I liked it or not, I was ready to be happy again. I had to do that for my kids. Both the boys' and my therapists advised that my sons would handle Jenn's death similarly to how I did, so I had to handle it as well as one possibly could. That didn't mean hiding my feelings, but I needed to get on with the business of living my life again, both for my own sake, and so the boys could follow my lead.

Not long after Jenn was hauled away in the van, I looked at my wedding band. It had been passed down from my grandparents. The one I wore was my grandfather's. He was a giant in my eyes, and I believe he was married to my grandmother for over thirty-five years. Ever since Jenn and I were having trouble in our early marriage, anytime I needed strength, I would look at that ring, think of him, and find a way to dig deeper. It was as if

I could borrow his strength by staring at the ring and remembering the great man he had been.

The band also represented seven and a half of the best years of my life, and sadly, two and a half of the worst. Looking at the ring then, I didn't focus on the negative, but recalled all the good times Jenn and I had shared together. Our entire marriage flashed before my eyes. Then the realization hit me:

My marriage is over. Jenn is gone, and I am a widower. My marriage is finished, complete, over and done.

People had told me I should take my time letting go of possessions with emotional ties to Jenn. Originally, I had planned to continue wearing my wedding band for however long I wanted to, but now I realized – there was no point in wearing it. Wedding rings are for married people, and I wasn't married anymore. Staring at it now brought me no peace of mind, only sadness. I got up, walked to the bedroom, removed the ring from my finger, and placed it in the sock and underwear drawer. I looked at it for another moment, not knowing if I would ever be ready to part with it. I was supposed to pass it down one day, after Jenn and I had bought our own rings, but we never did that. Still, my marriage was over, so I was done wearing it. At least I could gaze at our rings if I ever felt the need. With that, I closed the drawer and was done with it.

I have maybe worn it for a moment once or twice since then. My mom later asked about returning the rings to my grandmother – really, into my mom's safekeeping – so they could be passed down again, and I flipped out on her. That was when I realized how important they were to me. Of everything we had, those two rings, more than anything else, represented our marriage to me, and I definitely didn't want to let them go if I could help it. I had honestly thought I would be okay with returning them, but the moment my mom broached the subject, I lost it. She quickly agreed to let me keep them if that's what I wanted. It was. Just looking at the rings now brings back fond memories of my past life. Still, I wouldn't wear mine in public again.

Becky and I went for a walk later that night. I'm not sure what we talked about, but it was probably the huge sense of relief we each felt that Jenn's suffering had ended. There was no joy in either of our voices. We had survived the most emotionally challenging, exhausting, gut-wrenching experience in either of our lives. And Jenn didn't have to be in pain anymore.

Later I went to bed by myself, as a widower. There would be times when I had trouble falling asleep, but not that night. I hadn't closed my eyes for more than two hours in the past two days, and was physically and emotionally spent. So, I slept. It was the end of one life, and the next day marked the beginning of a new one.

There were several things that needed to be taken care of. We made multiple trips back and forth to San Angelo to deal with typical after-death business.

Visiting the funeral home was a surreal experience, as were most death related tasks. It's difficult to describe. I felt detached, with occasional twinges of sorrow. Most of it was hazy, like a dream, similar to when the doctors told us Jenn had cancer, but less surprising.

I struggled to keep up with everything the funeral home director was explaining about the services Jenn and her mom had pre-arranged. How the payment worked, what I needed to do for them, which included writing an obituary, signing paperwork, etc. I had a tough time putting my name on the paper to have Jenn cremated. It was what she had wanted, but giving away her body to be turned to ash was weird. I did my best to go through the motions, choosing to stay as detached as possible. But it wasn't always possible.

Condolence messages and phone calls overwhelmed me. The love and compassion from my family, friends and Jenn's followers was comforting, yet I felt distant. It never escaped me that, while we were receiving lots of love, it was only because Jenn was dead. I was grateful, but it felt bittersweet. Sometimes I read messages or spoke with people, and it seemed as if I wasn't really there. Updating Jenn's Facebook page to report her death was like that, as was publishing her goodbye video and typing up the accompanying message to her followers. I walked around the house like a ghost. I imagine a self-defense mechanism in the brain kicks in, so you don't become overwrought and have a mental breakdown, but I have no research to back that up.

After visiting the funeral home, I took care of another pressing issue. The thought of having to sleep in the bed Jenn died in, the bed the two of us had spent so much time in, was depressing. I wanted a new bed as part of my new life, but unfortunately, I couldn't afford one. I figured a new bed set would at least freshen things up and be better than nothing. My next stop was Bed, Bath & Beyond. I remember being in high school and going there with friends. We would gaze at the cool grown-up stuff and talk about our dream houses. Now here I was, ready to buy my own bedding for what I imagined would transform my room – as opposed to "our" room – and nothing caught my eye. I settled on a set I liked well enough. Why is nice bedding so expensive?

I can't remember if it was on that trip, but I also went to a local electronic cigarette shop. I didn't mention this in the first chapter, but Jenn and I were smokers when we met. We tried to quit numerous times and failed. When electronic cigarettes became available, we switched. It took us two years to fully convert from cigarettes to e-cigs, but we never regretted it. Our kids got sick less, we smelled better, everything tasted better, we could run better, sing better, coughed less and breathed easier. Although we never kicked the nicotine habit completely, we were proud of the fact that we quit smoking. It was one of many positive transformations we went through together.

So, I went to the e-cig shop. For months I had heard of these new and supposedly amazing kits called sub-ohm tanks. They create massive clouds of vapor, which I get a kick out of – don't ask me why, I just do. Although I didn't have a lot of money, my less responsible side told me I deserved a reward, having made it through the previous three weeks of increasing trauma. I asked for their best sub-ohm e-cig, and bought it.

I spent a bit too much on myself around that time. Before Jenn's condition had gotten really bad, I bought several upgrades for my computer. My Let's Play videos on YouTube had so far been produced in 720p resolution, and I wanted to step up my game to 1080p resolution in sixty frames per second. I purchased a high-end graphics card, memory upgrades, a better power supply unit and a solid-state drive. Opening the tower for the first time was an adventure, and I installed the parts myself. I screwed up transferring my operating system to the new drive, but a friend sorted that out for me after he visited for Jenn's memorial.

Consumerism doesn't help much. You buy stuff you don't really need, and although it feels good initially, it doesn't last, and is usually followed by guilt – at least in my case. Then again, maybe it does help a little bit. It helped Jenn, and it did distract me temporarily. Sometimes you do anything to lift your spirits. As long as you're not getting strung out on drugs or booze, cut yourself some slack. Besides, the computer upgrades were my very early Christmas present.

While I was at the funeral home and shopping, the boys got to go to Stephanie's gymnastics studio and play. They loved it, running around, doing stunts, being kids. It was a relief to see them having fun in light of their recent loss. The physical activity and joy were highly therapeutic. Thank you, Stephanie.

Essentially, while dealing with Jenn's after death matters, I was also changing my surroundings, if only in small ways, to symbolize my new and different life. I was tired of being depressed. Given the choice, Jenn would have never gotten sick, and I sincerely believe we would have been happily married until we were both old and gray. But that wasn't an option. I could either cling to my old life, which didn't exist anymore, or move on. I chose the latter.

Being so close to death triggered a powerful urge to live life in me. It was as if, upon seeing Jenn dying, a voice deep inside said, "Fuck that! I don't want to die! I want to live! I want to live as fully as possible!" I was anxious to escape the depression, and embrace my new reality, leaving death far behind. I had spent years among the walking dead. I did my time in hell. I had given my all to Jenn. Now I was ready to live again and be happy.

I am forever grateful to Becky and Cindy. The night Jenn died, Cindy went back home. She still managed to compose herself enough to assist with preparations for Jenn's memorial service. Becky took yet another week off work to help me with the boys and funeral arrangements. Becky, Stephanie, and a few other friends did the heavy lifting organizing the memorial service. Just as they had done during the last weeks of Jenn's life, they lightened my burden as much as possible. All I had to do was write the obituary and secure the venue.

We ended up having the memorial service at the local high school. They were very accommodating, and didn't charge us anything to use the auditorium. I'm extremely grateful for everything my school district administrators and colleagues did for my family throughout the almost three years of our cancer journey. From sick pools to fundraisers and moral support, they stood right behind us the entire time. You couldn't ask for a more considerate school district.

The boys and I needed suits for the memorial service. It meant another trip into town, spending more money, but it was worth it. I went to JC Penny while my mom took the boys to Dillard's, and by the end of our shopping spree, the three of us were looking quite dapper. Devin didn't dig the suit look, but Kayden loved it. He wears his every chance he gets, even around the house, pretending to be the president. I had wanted it to be a fun, positive experience, and it was. We left the mall that night looking sharp and feeling like a team. Team Cooper. I've been calling us that ever since.

Regardless of how much we had going on that week, we made sure to hang out and play with the kids, if they were up for it. Jenn died on a Thursday. I kept the boys home on Friday, but they seemed together enough to return to school on Monday, so I sent them. I had read it was important to maintain their routines if possible. They continued going to school, and our nighttime rituals didn't change. But we did give them extra attention to keep their mind off things.

The day Cindy picked up the urn, we met at the lake house where Jenn and I had gotten married. Several of Jenn's friends and family showed up. We went around the room sharing our fondest memories of her. Then everyone wrote a personal message to Jenn on a balloon, and went outside to release it into the air. This act was significant for the boys, especially for little Kayden. We all shed countless tears that day.

As it was getting dark and people were leaving, I took the urn and went to the exact spot where Jenn and I had exchanged our vows nearly ten years years before. I spoke to her while hugging the urn. Whether or not she could hear me, who knows. But something surprising happened. I felt as if Jenn was talking to me, internally. She was telling me she loved me, she wanted me to be happy, and to move on with my life. That night I learned that if I needed her advice, I simply had to be very still, wonder what Jenn would say, and eventually the answer would reveal itself to me. Through our intimate conversations over the past decade, I had gotten to know her that well. Not that anything in this first internal dialogue with Jenn was new, she had said it all to me before she died, several times. But this became my new relationship with her. If I desperately needed her, she was there, in my heart. I was carrying her with me, everywhere I went, always.

I waited until the last minute to write Jenn's obituary, hoping someone, anyone, would do it for me. How do you summarize someone's entire life in a few paragraphs? It seems impossible. I had read articles on composing a death notice, what to include and what to leave out. I decided to stay conventional and not get too creative. Once I had learned the essential elements of an obituary, most of it wrote itself. It wasn't as bad as I had made it out to be, but it wasn't fun either.

Having to write an obituary for Jenn was one of those punches I had to roll with. Like every time I had to tell someone who had not yet heard, that she was dead. Like at the e-cig shop, where Jenn randomly came up in conversation. The staff were talking about a regular customer fighting breast cancer, who was a super cool chick, and I had to say, "Yeah, that was my wife." Or when I first called myself a widower in public. I was being pummeled by little, unexpected jabs like that throughout the week. It sucked, but you adapt.

The day of the memorial service finally arrived after what felt like the longest week of my life. I had given myself two hours to get ready instead of the usual forty-five minutes, so I could make sure the boys were good to go, and to mentally prepare for the breakdowns I knew were coming. Team Cooper was ready.

I had no idea what the turnout would be. Jenn had a large following, but most of them didn't live in Texas. In the end it was mostly family and friends. The number of my family members and friends showing up surprised me. I hadn't done a great job of keeping in touch with them over the years, and yet they were there for me when I needed them the most. I was grateful for that.

The service was beautiful. Becky and a few of Jenn's friends had gone to the auditorium well in advance to test the projector, set up the flowers, a large wreath, and a portrait of Jenn, and to arrange the foyer. There was a guest book, an assortment of cookies and a gorgeous cake designed by our neighbor, who is a very talented baker.

I can't remember many details of the service. I recall being close to the boys and my parents. Due to Jenn's falling out with God, she had requested that if there was a pastor, they would only be allowed to lead one prayer, and could under no circumstances use this as an opportunity to convert people. I honestly have no clue if there was a pastor present or not, but I don't think so. Jeska, a gifted singer, performed a few songs, accompanied by a friend on guitar. We offered people the chance to speak. Becky, my dad, and I believe Cindy, gave moving speeches. I was proud of them. All week I had wanted to be able to go up and say something, but I never wrote anything down, and when the time came, I didn't have the strength to do it.

The slideshow got to me more than anything. Seeing images of our happy life together was painful. Even though I had grieved along the way, even though I had dealt with the loss better than I ever thought I would, it still hurt so much. We had shared such an incredible life and family. Despite most of it having been gone for a while, I still hated that it was lost forever.

At some point my mom left my side to comfort Cindy, who was having an even harder time than the boys and I. I couldn't blame her. Jenn had not only been her daughter, but her best friend. I can't imagine losing a child, much less an only child, and hope I never have to find out what that is like.

My mom and I after the memorial service.

Jenn had handpicked the music for her service, of which I remember only two songs. *Ghost of You* by My Chemical Romance and *The Show Must Go On* by Queen, which played at the very end of the ceremony. The message was clear. Jenn didn't want to be forgotten, but she didn't want us moping around forever, either. She had been feeling guilty about the pain her death would cause, hoping it wouldn't inflict too much damage to her friends and family. She needed us to move forward, and get busy living and being happy again. What an incredible final message. I took it to heart, and hope many others did, too.

Life started to pick back up, and I was ready for it. I felt stronger than ever, for several reasons.

I had fulfilled *all* of my wedding vows. Jenn and I had been together for better and worse, through sickness and health. We hadn't gotten rich, but we did climb out of poverty. We had started our relationship in my college apartment before spending a year in that tiny office trailer, unable to pay all our bills. By the time Jenn got sick, we had substantially improved our financial situation, and lived in a three-bedroom house which felt safe. That was close enough for me.

Most difficult of all, I stayed with her until death parted us. I had been a devoted and faithful husband to Jenn throughout the entirety of our marriage. While my best wasn't always good enough during the cancer journey, I gave her everything I had. Jenn knew that. Looking in the mirror, I felt a great sense of pride and accomplishment. "How many men at age thirty-one can say the same?" I wondered. I had proven to myself, beyond any doubt, that I was a good man.

It had only been a week or two since the most painful period of my life. I watched cancer slowly rip away every last piece of Jenn, including her memories, her grip on reality, her ability to communicate, and even her strength to so much as lift her arms off the bed for one final hug. It was damn hard, but I had pulled through. If I could get through that, I could probably get through anything life threw at me.

I experienced a combination of relief that Jenn's years of pain and suffering were over, and a sense of pride that I had helped her through it to the bitter end. There was a strong desire to step forward into this new life, to embrace it rather than run from it, and a determination to be happy again, backed by an inner strength I didn't know I had. I wonder if other widows and widowers feel the same. I hope they do.

As I was gradually putting the pieces of my new life together, I received support from an unexpected source, a gentleman I had never met before, by the name of Chad. Chad messaged me on Facebook one day. He told me he had been where I was now about a year prior, and had promised Jenn he would reach out to me after her death. I gladly accepted his offer. We set up a regular time to call, and spoke on the phone every Tuesday evening for at least a few months.

Chad was an incredible grief mentor. Like Angel, he gave me hope that I would do alright as a single dad, that my kids would be fine, and that I could be happy and even find love again. Chad was a pro. In his free time, he liked helping other widowers get through the initial stages after death. I was lucky to receive counsel from a guy like that.

The conversations with Chad were invaluable to me. Each week, new emotions, ideas or issues came up. Be it positive new developments or intense feelings of guilt, Chad was able to relate to it all. He was the navigator, helping me sail through choppy waters, rooting me on. We've fallen out of touch now, but that's fine. It frees him up to focus on his new family, and help someone else who needs him more. We will always be cheering for each other.

Chad invited me into widow/widower support groups on Facebook. Jenn had tried to get me to join caregiver support groups, but I couldn't do it back then. I would read horror stories of patients in hospice, and couldn't stomach it. But as a widower, I found the groups quite helpful. People talk about still missing their spouse. They share good days and bad days alike. I highly recommend joining a support group, but it can be difficult to get into one. The main one I'm active in is *LNWW Late Night Widows & Widowers*, which is by invite only. Every member must be vetted and approved by the admin to verify their new and unfortunate marital status. But I get why they do it. It's imperative to keep the group a safe and intimate place, even though it has several thousand members.

I stayed home for a week or two after Jenn died. By the time I returned to work, I could hold myself together pretty well. It was easier not to think about Jenn when I was teaching, because it required all my focus. Continuing to work had been a good coping mechanism for me throughout the cancer journey. I did have moments of weakness, but fortunately Adrian was there to cover for me if I couldn't pull it together for my next class, which happened several times. Sometimes, even at work, you have to go to a safe place and let yourself cry it out. Eventually you will calm down, and then you can get back to it.

As a band director, you constantly worry whether your band is making adequate progress. Most teachers' objective is to ensure their students pass the state standardized test. For band directors, it's all about getting them ready for contests. In Texas – and a few other states – we put a tremendous amount of pressure on ourselves. The standards for achieving the best rating at the state-run contests are very high. Your band has to sound "near flawless," and have a mature or close to professional sound. My middle-schoolers are not professionals, but considering the music they are playing, it's expected they sound like pros. It is incredibly hard to do. We spend all year training our students to become strong enough musicians in time for their performance. I hadn't been stressing about the band for quite some time as other things had taken priority, but I was elated to hear the amazing progress they had achieved under Adrian's direction while I was gone. As a bonus, the kids felt bad for me, so they were better-behaved than usual.

It was similar for the boys with school, both while Jenn was sick and after she died. Their teachers were well aware of our situation and gave them the space – or privacy, in Devin's case – to cry when they needed to. They had full access to the school's counselor, and she helped them through their breakdowns. Everyone at the elementary school was wonderful with the boys. We are truly lucky to have had such caring and understanding teachers and faculty.

I had three goals in my new life. The first was to completely purge, clean and reorganize the house, to make it "mine". Secondly, I wanted to lose some weight and regain my physical strength. My greatest desire was to get my finances in order. Despite dreading it, I had to continue working on death-related tasks, such as removing Jenn from my accounts, reporting her death to various places, file a life insurance claim, and whatever else I didn't even know about or had forgotten.

I started by focusing on the house, because I had promised Devin it would become more organized, clean and neat after his mom's death. I needed to make good on that, for him and for myself. The plan was to prioritize the most used and visible rooms. My closets and Jenn's dresser were at the very bottom of the list.

I was working on the house whenever I could, typically on the weekend, or anytime I felt motivated. During the week, if I had an extra hour before cooking dinner, I would start tackling the corner of a room, for example, and finish it up after we ate. To avoid getting overwhelmed, I picked small spaces to organize at a time. Clearing off the dining room table was one task, the shelving unit next to it another. I purged everything we didn't use, unless it had a deep sentimental value. In determining what to keep and what to get rid of, I asked myself, "Does it add happiness and value to your life? If so, hold onto it. If not, throw it out." That's what I did.

Within a couple of months I had made it through the main areas of the house aside from Kayden's room, my closets – including Jenn's old closet – and Jenn's dresser. Our home was transformed, which not only made it easier to relax in for me, but Devin truly appreciated it. The house felt more like mine now, since everything in it was there because I wanted it to be.

Losing weight wasn't as difficult as expected. I had already dropped fifteen pounds by preparing healthy dinners. I still hate cooking. It takes forty minutes to an hour for five minutes of pleasure.

Feeding my family is satisfying, though, especially when they enjoy the food. I encouraged the boys to be vocal and give me honest feedback on my cooking. They typically liked what I made, but if they didn't, they told me why. I used this information to cater to their taste buds, so now they think everything I cook is the bomb.

Sitting in a box in the garage, collecting dust, was a workout bench I had bought months earlier, after my therapist recommended I start exercising. While cleaning the dining room area, I created a tiny space for it, and finally put it together. More importantly, I began using it. It took a while to establish a routine and stick with it, but for a couple of months I was working out consistently. Then I missed a week, skipped another one, and, well, you know how it goes. I'm hoping to get back on the horse soon, though.

My financial situation was a train wreck. There were many issues to sort out, student loans, bad credit, paying off the car, applying for social security income death benefits, filing Jenn's life insurance policy claim, and more. There is a saying, "How do you move a mountain? One rock at a time." That's how I approached this. I started somewhere and focused on one task at a time.

I did make one investment despite my shaky finances, but I believe it will be worth it. We joined the Disney Vacation Club. It's like a timeshare, except you purchase a certain number of points, which you can use at any Disney resort or affiliated location all over the world. Each room is worth a fixed number of points per night, so you can spend yours to stay wherever you like. Without going into the math, I can assure you that if you want to go on Disney vacations regularly – which we totally do – it saves you thousands of dollars in the long run.

I spent the remaining money Jenn's family, friends and followers had donated to us for after death expenses on the down payment. Due to my bad credit history I only qualified for their smallest package, and that was after my representative, who knew our story, pulled some strings. But we got in. We don't have enough points for an annual Disney vacation, but every other year we can get a small, double queen room for seven days and nights at certain resorts, and it's already paid for the next twenty-four years. Hopefully I'll be able to add more points someday, so we can either book a suite or go every year.

Otherwise, I was trying to be a responsible adult. I started by creating a monthly budget. My last attempt was in college when Jenn shot it down, and I was excited to give it a proper chance this time. I retrieved a bank statement and used it to estimate my typical expenses and monthly bills, then wrote everything down on a budget sheet I got from Dave Ramsey's *Total Money Makeover* book. I set spending goals and eliminated wasteful spending. Any extra cash I used to overpay my debts, among other things. If you need to get your finances in order, I highly recommend that book.

I adopted the envelope system for the first few months. You withdraw all the money you're going to spend for a certain period from the bank, then divvy it up among several labeled envelopes. For example, I would put six hundred dollars in the "Groceries" envelope, and then try to only spend that amount on groceries for the month. It was an easy way to see how much money we had left in each category. I stopped using the system once I felt confident in my spending habits. I now use Dave Ramsey's budget app, called EveryDollar, to easily create monthly budgets and track my spending. I haven't had a perfect month yet where everything went according to plan, but these days that just means I only had *some* money instead of a bunch of money to put toward debt. Since making a budget and sticking to it, there is always cash left over at the end of the month, which I use to get us out of debt.

One day that money will go toward retirement. The point of doing all this work to manage my finances and get out of debt is so I can retire a multi-millionaire. Being a public school teacher, that would be quite a feat. It would mean living well below my means for the next three-plus decades, but it's possible. How amazing would that be? If I die early, my kids will get everything I saved, so it's good regardless of what happens.

Once the social security death benefit was set up, I used some of that money to start college savings accounts for Devin and Kayden. I wish we would've done this a long time ago. We had always wanted to, but never managed our finances well enough. Even when Jenn was receiving disability checks, and we had extra money, she was intimidated by the task of setting it up, and I was always at work during business hours. It finally got done, though. It's not much right now, because most spare money goes toward debt, but we'll contribute more each month when we can. Even so, it's still a lot more than my family had saved up for my college tuition. Not that I'm criticizing them. I'm a first generation college graduate, and it's common for parents who didn't attend or finish college to either not think about it or not be able to do it.

I had invested a small amount into a Fidelity Roth IRA for myself, just to get something started. And by small amount, I mean fifty dollars. However, after a few months I decided to stop and redirect that money to paying off debt, too, as Dave Ramsey suggests. Once I finish building up our emergency fund, I'll be able to put several hundred dollars a month in there, which is what it will take for me to retire a multi-millionaire. For now though, I need to throw everything I've got at the stupid debt. But I can't wait to start putting it into the IRA and getting to see my retirement savings balance climb.

I enjoy crunching money numbers. It's like a game to me, and one I very much want to win. I'm not interested in taking on extra work and losing valuable time with my family, so I'm trying to optimize our spending with the income I'm already generating. I don't know why I think that's fun, but I do. The only time I get stressed out is when we go more than one hundred dollars over budget, which doesn't happen very often.

My credit score became a bit of an obsession. Every month I logged into several credit monitoring websites, as they get their data from different credit bureaus, and use varying algorithms to calculate the final number. Anytime my score went up, I cheered. Eventually, I applied for and received my first credit cards. Dave Ramsey does not recommend them, but I wanted to benefit from cash back rewards. I use rewards cards for almost everything, generating an extra fifty dollars a month.

Most importantly, I pay off my cards every week. I'm very careful not to spend money I don't have. If I can't afford it, there's no way I'm buying it. I refuse to add to my debt. The good news is that my credit score has climbed over one hundred points this past year, from the 620's to just over 730. I officially have good credit.

Handling after death matters was an ongoing process. Death certificates are required to do anything, so I had to apply and wait for them to show up. Then I was able to update the Social Security Administration and confirm arrangements for the death benefits. I had always supported our family on my income alone, which is why we could barely get by. When Jenn received her disability benefit, she used it to buy fun things to keep everyone's spirits up. Since I wasn't spending it that way, it effectively boosted our household income. I'm certainly grateful for it.

Jenn's life insurance took a surprisingly long time to get processed – a couple of months at least. I repaid Cindy for my part of the cremation and memorial service costs, and spent the rest to pay off our car. Jenn had advised me to use the money that way, and I'm glad I did. I love not having a car payment.

I was reluctant to remove Jenn from our joint checking and savings account. I'm not sure why I was dreading it so much. Perhaps because it was one of the last legal ties that still bound us together. However, it had been causing me problems without my knowledge.

Every month, the school district direct deposited my paycheck, and each time it was put on hold for an extra day or two. After a few months of this, I investigated why it kept happening.

Apparently depositing a check into an account with a dead person listed flags the transaction, so the bank has to review it before allowing it to clear. Upon learning this, I knew I had to finally remove Jenn from the accounts. I dragged myself to the bank one morning, death certificate in hand. It wasn't fun. I choked up a bit. But I got it done.

You have to take these tasks on one at a time and try to not let yourself get overwhelmed. You will get them all done eventually.

My entire adult life I had put off drafting a will. I knew having a will was important, yet I never did until after Jenn died. Jenn never created a will. She just told her inner circle what she was leaving them, and how she wanted the rest of her stuff handled. I felt I needed more protection. The illusion that I would live forever was stripped from me when I watched Jenn slowly dying. Life is fragile, and while I promised my kids I'll be around until I'm an old man, there's no guarantee that will be the case.

I went to LegalZoom.com and used their service to draft up a will, then had it witnessed and notarized. I asked one of my best friends to be the executor of my will once I'm gone, and told him where I keep the relevant documents. Having a non-family member carry out my will made sense to me, in case there are conflicts or arguments, and because that way none of my family members have to be in the hot seat. If someone gets mad at my friend, that's fine, but I don't want anyone in the family to have to take any heat if there are disagreements with my will.

The boys bounced back pretty well. They didn't experience the kind of personal growth period I had, but we did have one feeling in common. While they missed mom, they were glad she wasn't in pain anymore. We said that to each other on a regular basis.

We continued therapy through the end of the following summer. The boys' therapist was impressed with how well they were doing, as was mine.

I kept their routines the same, including our Family Night tradition of eating pizza and watching The Flash or a movie. The nighttime procedure never changed, either, but I tried to add a new ritual. We had set up Jenn's urn, a few pictures and flowers on the entertainment center in the living room. On the first of each month, we circled up next to her altar, and I would say, "Well, it's been one more month since your mom died. How do you feel? How do you think we're doing?" I wanted to gauge their disposition and give them an opportunity to open up about it. Then we each shared a good memory about mom.

I honestly don't know if this was helpful or not, but I had read it could provide comfort for children. We stuck with it for three months, and on the first day of the fourth month, they were having so much fun with their friends that I decided to let them keep playing. They hadn't realized it was the monthly anniversary of their mother's death. I figured having fun was probably just as therapeutic.

As promised, I let the boys romp around all over the house again. Friends could come over, hang out in the living room and play video games with the volume turned up. Devin got to have sleepovers. This was a huge boost to the boys' morale.

Just a few weeks after Jenn's death, we had to face our first Christmas without her. Chad's advice was, "Make some time for yourself, after presents, to go to your room, and cry it out for as long as you need to." I planned on doing that.

Christmas morning went well, even in Jenn's absence. Kayden was thrilled Santa had come, and Devin was excited about the presents, despite knowing who the real Santa was. They loved their gifts, and had a blast with them like every other Christmas. We were hosting that year, and I had just started plating food, when I felt the grief rush over me. If I'm honest, it had been bothering me that Jenn wasn't there. I tried to focus on the boys, and be in the now. They were enjoying the magic of Christmas morning, but I was struggling.

My dad walked into the kitchen and asked if he could help with anything. I told him I needed to be alone to cry it out, and would he mind serving the food. I had several good, hard cries that day. After each one, I felt better, and was able to rejoin the family and enjoy myself. Until the next wave hit. At the end of the day, Devin said, "This was the best Christmas ever!" Kayden agreed. I was surprised and relieved to hear that. They each did have moments when they wished their mom was there, but neither of them broke down the way I did. For that, I was grateful.

We had survived the first of many "firsts," and in doing so, thanks to Chad's advice, I had learned how to cope and get through the others. First birthdays, Father's Day, Mother's Day, wedding anniversary, Thanksgiving, Easter, school programs, the list goes on. If I knew I might get emotional, I made sure to have an escape plan for when and where I could cry it out. Sometimes I did have to openly weep, even if the boys saw it. That was okay. I wanted them to know I was missing their mom, too, and understood, at least to some degree, what they were going through. My kids are the best at consoling me when I'm sad about Jenn.

I specifically didn't mention mom on special days, waiting instead to see if they brought her up. If they did, I would hold and console them, emphasizing that Jenn had done everything she possibly could have to stay with us. I reiterated how much mom had loved them, and how proud she would be to see them now. On most occasions, including both their birthdays, the boys didn't seem to notice Jenn's absence. If they were having fun, I certainly didn't want to ruin that by reminding them of their loss.

More than a year later, I still experience regular episodes of grief. They are not as frequent and less intense now, but marked by crying fits and a deep sense of sorrow. Anything can trigger me. Sometimes there is no trigger at all. Over the two years and nine months of Jenn's battle with cancer I had gotten used to these incidents, learning not to judge them as bad, but as healing, and therefore positive events. They were inconvenient, but necessary to get better and move on.

Emotional pain comes in waves. It starts out as giant swells, washing over you in quick succession, knocking you off your feet. As time progressed, they happened further apart and were easier to ride out. I went from having one episode a day, to a few days without one, then an entire week.

During an episode you cry, think you're pulling it together, and a minute later it's back to bawling. You're being tossed like a ship on turbulent waters. Try to relax and allow yourself to be sad. Know this moment won't last forever, let it run its course, and give yourself permission to grieve. It's essential for healing.

Generally speaking, I felt good. A massive weight had been lifted from my shoulders. I was stronger than ever, and trying to take this opportunity to grow and be a better person. When the breakdowns came, I didn't mind them. Crying had become an old friend. Letting it all out allowed me to return to whatever I was doing with more focus. I had proven to myself I could handle being a single dad and enjoy life without Jenn.

Chapter 11

Into Happiness

"The sun will rise again."

– CHUCK NOLAND, *CAST AWAY*

I WAS CONVINCED it would be nearly impossible to find love after Jenn. There wasn't anyone in our circle I was interested in. I couldn't see myself hooking up with another band director or coworker. Perhaps I would get lucky and meet a cool girl on Minecraft, but female gamers are pretty rare, and spread all over the world. The odds of finding a compatible life partner seemed abysmal. I certainly didn't expect that the person I would fall in love with had, indeed, been right in front of me all along.

If you guessed Becky, Jenn's best friend and the boys' godmother, you are correct. Jenn herself had tried to set us up before she died. Becky had always been an excellent godmother to Devin and Kayden. During her visits with Jenn, she often set aside extra time to spend with just them. Becky was such a skilled parental figure that we were completely comfortable with her correcting the boys' behavior as she saw fit.

Jenn early on realized we had a lot in common, primarily that Becky grew up in the band world. Once, her dad's band was selected as the top band in the state for its classification. Becky had been in the band through most of college. She had marched color guard in Drum Corps International – the major league of marching band, and continues to teach color guards, although she chose to major in history instead of music. We have a lot of other things in common we didn't even know about back then. But Jenn did.

She wanted both of us to be happy after she was gone. For Becky to finally be with a good guy, and I was the best guy Jenn knew. She wanted me to end up with a great woman, and Becky was the best woman she knew. Becky loved the boys. I think for Jenn the solution was glaringly obvious. So, she got to work.

Jenn had talked to me about Becky on multiple occasions. "You know," she would start, "I think after I'm dead, you should give Becky a try." What an awkward conversation. Each time I reiterated that I wasn't interested in Becky and just didn't see it. Jenn kept pointing out our commonalities, but I found the whole idea too strange to even consider, and remained unreceptive. Jenn was insistent, though, and may have planted a seed.

When she talked to Becky about this, she was even more relentless. "You should try to hook up with Chris after I'm gone." Becky always reacted with shock and disbelief. But Jenn continued, explaining how much we had in common, and that I was a great guy. Becky said she knew I was a great guy, but just wasn't interested.

Jenn enjoyed making people feel embarrassed. It was funny to her. Once, in front of a group of friends, Jenn was discussing what she was leaving to whom. Then, with a devilish smile, she looked at Becky and said, "And I'm leaving something *very* special to Becky..."

"You can't will me your husband!" Becky shouted back.

A few times, when all three of us were hanging out, Jenn said that we should hook up, but *only* after she was dead. Neither Becky or I had any desire to, and it was just a weird topic and extremely uncomfortable.

Jenn even went so far as telling her mom she was hoping Becky and I would end up together. If there was anyone Jenn could trust with the boys and me, it was Becky. I didn't find out about these conversations until after Becky and I were dating, and that's when I realized how much Jenn had been wanting this.

Regardless, that's not why we ended up together. I honestly had no secret intentions for Becky. Something must have changed when she was helping with Jenn's end of life care. After we had made it through that, my respect and admiration for her were at an all-time high. I had seen her be a devoted nurse to Jenn, taking on some of the most difficult tasks, always ready to jump in when she saw I was distressed or exhausted. She was, simply, amazing.

Our connection deepened when we started talking more often. I met Becky approximately five months before Jenn. She had transferred to my college, joined the band, and been a member of Kappa Kappa Psi, National Honorary Band Fraternity. Although we had spent a decent amount of time around each other, mostly for band and fraternity activities, I never got to know her well. She was Jenn's best friend, not mine.

The week following Jenn's death, while preparing for the memorial service, Becky and I saw each other every day. We kept going on our walks, except now we didn't have to vent about Jenn's suffering anymore. We did express how much we were missing her, but talked about other topics, too. I told her I knew I could never be her replacement for Jenn, that I would probably make a very poor substitute, but that I was happy to try to be a new best friend for her, if she was up for it. She didn't seem very comforted by the gesture, but it marked a new beginning for us. After Becky had returned home, we continued checking in on each other. Before long we were chatting daily, typically at the end of the day, after the boys were tucked in.

As I was getting to know Becky better, I started to develop feelings for her. This caught me by complete surprise. Hardly any time had passed since Jenn's death, so how could I possibly have a romantic interest in someone else? When I brought this up to Becky, she admitted to feeling the same way, and was just as astonished. Maybe it was simply a manifestation of our shared grief, or a temporary affection caused by having gone through an extremely difficult situation together. We decided to wait and see.

Some time passed, and not a day went by without hearing from each other, even if it was just a quick text message. We enjoyed our phone conversations, but were eager to hang out in person again. The next weekend my mom was watching the boys, I made plans to visit Becky.

Meanwhile, the idea of dating Becky had grown on me. I was still quite uncertain about it all, and didn't trust my own intuition, so I asked Misty for advice. I knew she wouldn't judge me, but I was judging myself. The traditional mourning period for a widower is one year, and people often wait longer than that. My grief mentor, Chad, had found his fiancé several months after the death of his wife, so maybe I could be ready for love sooner, too.

During my next session with Misty I cautiously broached the subject. I explained that Becky and I had known each other for over ten years, and how much we had in common. Becky was working at a juvenile treatment facility and finishing up her teacher certification. Jenn and I had been an "opposites attract" couple, whereas Becky and I have similar personalities and values, in addition to our shared interests.

"Wow, it sounds like you're practically the same person!" Misty said with a big smile on her face.

"So then, what do I do? Do I keep waiting? Or do you think I would be okay if I go for it now?" I fully trusted Misty's professional opinion and intimate knowledge of not just the past year, but my entire life. Whatever she recommended would be in my best interest.

"If this were literally anyone else, I would tell you to put the brakes on. But because it's Becky, because of your history, her relationship with the boys, her friendship with Jenn, the fact that she understands better than anyone else what you're going through, because she's grieving the loss of the same person, because of everything that's established there, I would say, if you're ready, then it's okay. But only if you're ready."

I agreed with her assessment. I don't think this could've happened so soon with anyone *other* than Becky. However, this was begging my next question, "How do I know if I'm ready?"

Misty considered her words carefully, then said, "If you feel like you're ready, then you probably are. You've shown incredible judgment, so I trust that you'll make the right decision for you and the boys. So, when you feel ready, then you are."

I was starting to get excited. "You don't think it's too soon?"

She paused, then simply said, "Only do this if you really think you can handle it, and if you feel like you're ready to let someone else into your heart. At the same time, don't hold yourself back based on someone else's idea of a timeline."

I felt ready. Because I felt ready, timelines be damned.

I had been working hard on improving myself, my surroundings, the entire direction of my life. I was capable on my own, and a decent single dad. I had nothing more to prove to myself or anybody else. I felt strong. I hated being single. A wife is an integral part of my dream life, and I wanted to chase that dream again. That meant giving a relationship with Becky a shot. It felt right, and I decided to trust my instincts. Usually, I get into trouble when I'm *not* listening to my heart.

The next time I saw Becky in person I told her what my therapist had said. She was still worried about it being too soon, which I understood. I wasn't in a rush, and certainly wasn't going to pressure her into anything. We moved on to other topics.

Something changed the following night. We sat on the couch watching the show "Arrow", because we're both superhero nerds. At some point, Becky leaned into me. I waited a moment to see if she would recoil, but she stayed, so I placed my arm around her. I commented with an unsure voice, "Thanks. It's nice to know we're on cuddling terms, I guess."

After a while it started to bug me. I blurted out, "You know, I don't just cuddle with friends. That's not really a friend thing to me."

"Yeah, I know..." Becky replied in a disappointed voice. I wasn't sure if it was disappointment in herself, or because she was feeling uncomfortable with the idea of being with me, but she surely sounded disappointed.

"So, I think either we should be together, or we shouldn't be doing this." I continued.

"I know. I don't know what to do." Becky replied with a hint of struggle in her voice.

"Well, I'm not putting any pressure on you. But if you want to be together, then let's be together." Never had I been so calm when asking a woman out, not even Jenn, who had said yes before I could ask.

After a long silence, she finally said, "Okay."

"Okay?" I asked, smiling. To this day I am teasing Becky for her underwhelming response.

She looked up at me and nodded, "Okay."

"Okay!" I said, and leaned in for our first kiss. It was spectacular.

Becky and I on our first date.

Once Becky and I had started our relationship, we needed to figure out how and when to tell everyone. We were nervous because it had been less than a year since Jenn's death. Less than six months, even. People were bound to question my judgment or Becky's intentions. We also had an online community to think of. Those paying attention knew Jenn wanted me to move on and be happy. Her inner circle was well aware she had hoped it would be with Becky. But I feared the timing would be hard to swallow for many. Not that it was anyone else's business, but this was one of the downsides to sharing our journey in public.

Hiding the relationship was not an option. I was proud and excited to be with Becky, and confident we would work out. In the end we agreed to tell our family right away, then Cindy, then the boys, then everyone else.

All of our family were receptive. My dad's reaction surprised me, "Thank God!" he exclaimed, "I actually prayed for this to happen!" That was sweet of him. Then he said, "Tell her, Welcome to the family" Whoa, I thought, we're not quite there yet. Maybe he saw how it would play out before I could. My mom and grandmother had serious concerns about the timing, but ultimately trusted my judgment. Above all, they wanted me to be happy. Becky's parents were also apprehensive about the timing and whether it could potentially hurt Becky or the boys. But they believed I was a good guy and as long as their daughter was happy, they were on board. Within a week, our immediate family was informed and supported us.

We waited a while longer to tell Cindy. She was still devastated by Jenn's loss, and we wanted to be respectful of that. What if we made her feel worse? We held off for a few weeks, until one day Becky went ahead and told her. Cindy was so happy for us, revealing how Jenn had talked to her about this, and that she and Charles hoped I would end up with Becky. If anyone could love the boys as much as Jenn, they thought, it would be her.

Devin and Kayden were next. I didn't want to do anything that might hurt or elongate their grieving process, so I consulted their therapist. "The boys are ready," she said. "They've both talked to me about how they'll have a new mom someday. It sounds like their mom talked to them a lot about it. So no, I don't think you'll hurt their healing process by being in a relationship." I was relieved. I didn't like keeping it from them. "Just be careful," she advised, "It will be natural for them to think of the next woman you bring into their life as being their next mother. So just try to be really sure about that person before you tell them."

I thought about that. Once Becky and I were together, it was wonderful. I remember doubting there would ever be room in my heart for another woman besides Jenn. Now I realized I could keep a place in my heart for Jenn, and still have plenty of space to fall in love with someone else.

Falling in love again, I had forgotten how amazing and thrilling that was. After a few weeks I felt sure I wanted to marry Becky. I didn't propose for a while, but I knew. It reminded me of how quickly my relationship with Jenn had escalated. Back then, all of my friends told me we were moving too fast, that I should slow down, but I never wavered. My feelings for Becky were the same I had for Jenn more than ten years ago. It felt wonderful, and right, and I was going to trust my instincts.

As soon as the boys' therapist confirmed they were ready, I set it up. After our respective therapy sessions, we went to the mall, and I bought ice cream. While we were sitting there, eating ice cream and watching people skate on the ice rink, I broke the news to them.

"So, do ya'll want to hear something really cool?" I asked.

"What's that?" Devin replied.

"I... have a girlfriend!" I said excitedly. They both looked at me wide-eyed.

Devin asked in shock, "Really?" Kayden echoed him, tone of voice included.

"Yes, really!" I said.

"Who is it? What is she like?" Devin was obviously leading this inquisition.

"It's someone you know. Can you guess who it is?" They went through everyone they could think of, except for Becky, eventually giving up.

"It's Becky!"

After a moment of contemplation, Devin said, with disappointment, "Aww, man! I mean, don't get me wrong, Becky is cool. I was just kind of hoping for someone else, you know? Someone new."

"Yeah," Kayden said, "I wanted it to be someone new!"

"Really? But you boys love Becky! And you already know she'll be nice to you. I thought ya'll would be excited for that."

Devin and Kayden reiterated their point. Fortunately, thirty minutes later, as we were getting back on the road, the boys had changed their minds and were now happy about Becky being my girlfriend. They immediately wondered if she was their new mom, to which I responded, "Not yet, but hopefully someday, if things keep going well." They had questions about the timeline, the dating process, how it was all going to happen.

Their entire lives had been with their birth parents, so they had never seen an actual courtship play out before, and legitimately didn't know anything about how it worked or what to expect.

"Why can't you just get married already?" Kayden said. He was very anxious to have a new mom. Within days of Jenn's death, he was expecting me to deliver this new mom that Jenn told him would one day show up. He wanted a mom so bad. Even now that he has a better understanding of how long these things can take, he will ask me, "Why can't ya'll just get married now?"

The boys acted sheepishly the next time they saw Becky in person, but quickly got past that. Becky and I were relieved we could openly be a couple around them.

Once the boys knew, we didn't wait long to make it public. As I'm writing this, I still haven't changed my Facebook status from Widower. I'm proud to be a widower. I'm not happy I'm a widower, but I wear it like a badge of honor. It says that I didn't shirk from my wedding vows. Both Becky and I posted a picture of us together on our private pages, and started letting our other friends know about us. Everyone was very supportive, which surprised me.

There was minor blowback within the Coffee With Coop community, but only from a few followers. Most reactions were positive. Some people didn't understand it, but were okay with it, while a handful were disgusted and thought that not only was it too soon but also disrespectful to Jenn. Other followers came to my defense, explaining that if they watched Jenn's videos, this was exactly what she had wanted. They felt I was doing right by Jenn and the boys. Kisha, Jenn's cancer sister and site moderator, eventually deleted those comment threads, so I didn't have to continue to justify myself to people who were never going to get it anyway.

It helped to have a couple of friends in the comments, including Kisha, who had witnessed Jenn harassing Becky about hooking up with me after she was dead. They vouched for me, that not only had Jenn wanted me to move on, but with Becky, specifically. I can understand the idea seemed preposterous to a lot of people – Becky and I had rejected it for a long time ourselves – but other cancer patients wrote about trying to do the same for their husbands.

The valid concern friends and followers brought up was the potential impact on Devin and Kayden. I reassured everybody I was being extremely careful in this regard, pointing out the lengths Jenn had gone to to prepare the boys, how I had waited to tell them until I had their therapist's approval and was sure the relationship with Becky was going to last. That appeared to quell most of the doubters.

Once everyone knew, a huge weight fell off our shoulders. Becky and I could openly be together, be happy about it, and not worry about what anyone might think. Being in a relationship so soon after Jenn's death was incredibly stressful, but love is worth it.

Not long after Becky and I had started dating, I began to feel strange about the relationship. I couldn't put my finger on it. Nothing obvious had changed, but internally there was a shift. A stressful feeling I couldn't identify, which was getting in the way of my ability to enjoy our time together. Becky was patient and understanding. She talked with me about it, tried to help me figure it out, gave me the space I needed to process, and permission to have those doubts. It was exactly the response I needed. After enough time and self-reflection, I concluded it was guilt. I had let someone else into my heart. A nagging feeling told me Becky wasn't the one I was supposed to be with. It was Jenn, and only Jenn.

Chad said the same had happened to him, and he guided me through it. I had to repeat affirmations to myself. I had fulfilled my wedding vows to the absolute fullest. I had done right by Jenn and continued to act in accordance with her wishes. I was doing the best for my sons, and we had the support of our family and friends. At last I felt ready to be happy. I wouldn't say I deserved it. Whether or not you deserve something in life is meaningless in many respects. I felt confident I was a good man, and that I had done everything I could for Jenn. Jenn wasn't coming back. So then, there was no reason to stop myself from experiencing bliss with Becky. Once I went through this thought process, my guilt subsided.

Being with Becky added so much happiness to my life. Falling in love with her reminded me of what it was like to fall in love with Jenn. I remembered more of the good times, rather than focusing on the hell we had endured. Granted, the happy memories were also difficult. I was still grieving the life I had lost. But that got better. Nowadays, when I think of Jenn, I see her the way she had been before cancer, and that's how I like to remember her.

Having Becky around has been good for the boys. Kayden really misses having a mom, and Devin is excited, too. He loves Becky. They talk regularly, and she's able to counsel him better than I can. Becky is not only perceptive and empathetic, but thanks to her training at the treatment center, she has a thorough understanding of issues kids deal with, and knows how to coach them through those. Which is hugely beneficial for Devin, whose anger issues still rear their ugly head from time to time.

While being with Becky reminds me of the good times with Jenn, the relationship itself is not at all similar. We have a very different dynamic, and I like that. I didn't have many interests in common with Jenn. Becky and I are both nerds, which I love. She's not much of a gamer, and I'm not a history buff, but those are our main differences. Jenn and I were attracted to each other in part because we shared a common background. We were both only children to single parents, spent much of our lives at the poverty level, and experienced the effects of drugs and alcoholism in our families. Becky's upbringing was nothing like that. Her birth parents are still living together and she has two siblings. Yet our personalities are very similar. We both tend to to stay calm and collected. Our sense of humor is alike, and we share the same goals in life. Learning about Becky, and about us as a couple, has been such a joyous experience.

My goal for the year after Jenn's death was to take the boys on our first real vacation without mom. I wanted to do something grand, like Disney, in hopes it would keep them entertained so they wouldn't have to think about Jenn so much.

However, having handled the boys on my own the year before, I wanted to bring someone else along. I thought about asking my parents, but I could only afford to take one person, so whom would I pick? Would the other parent feel slighted? I didn't want to risk that. Cindy was out, because in her condition, it would mean having one more person to take care of, and I would be worn out from the boys. That left Becky, who happily agreed. She had never been to a Disney park before, and was excited for it.

My Disney Vacation Club membership covered the resort stay, but that still left plane tickets, park tickets, and meals. Becky pitched in as much as she could, and I paid for one item per month. First the plane tickets, then meals, then park admission.

I won't say much about that trip, except for a few details. We did have a great time, though it just wasn't the same. The boys and I felt Jenn's absence. We tried not thinking about it, but that didn't always work.

One evening, at Hollywood Studios, we went to a new attraction they had added since our previous visit. It was a live concert by a small symphony orchestra performing medleys from the best Disney/Pixar films. The show was wonderful. The symphony orchestra played with precision and musical expression. While they performed, a "best of" montage was shown on a projector for each film's franchise, and the music was scored to go along with the images on screen. Pixar characters appeared on stage, and giant, green toy soldiers ushered you to your seat. I was triggered when they started performing the music from *Up*. The film's protagonist was a widower, and Jenn and I had loved that movie. Seeing the backstory of how he loved and lost his wife did me in. I had to leave after that performance and returned later when I had collected myself.

It wasn't always this dramatic. Anything we had done with Jenn the time before was tough. Thankfully, there is a *lot* to do at Disney World, and it's easy to find new areas to explore, so we focused on those.

We stayed at a different resort, and that helped. Although, because we were in a double queen bedroom with no dividers, Becky and I never got a break from the boys, which was exhausting at times. The resort itself – Disney's Animal Kingdom – Jambo House – was awesome. It's located inside the savanna reservation, where all the animals roam free. Walking outside, you saw giraffes and zebras, along with numerous other kinds of African animals. They were fenced in, but you could get very close. It was incredible.

Devin, Kayden and Becky with Goofy.

This being my third Disney trip, I had gotten the hang of how to do it right. We dined a lot with the characters, for example. My tip, if you're staying at a Disney resort, take advantage of the "Extra Magic Hours." The park stays open longer for resort guests only, which means much shorter lines. We took the boys to the recently opened Pandora – World of Avatar. While that place is cool during the day, it's bioluminescent at night, and gorgeous.

Magic Kingdom had extra magic hours another night, so Becky and I hired a babysitter, and went on a date. It was a fun and romantic night. Perhaps more importantly, with the exception of the Haunted Mansion, it was so different from my time there with Jenn that I didn't get sad thinking about it.

Overall, the trip was a success. My only regret was not having enough money to take the boys to Legoland for a day. I had promised I would bring them back, and apologized for not being able to do it this time. They both said it was fine, acknowledging how lucky they were to return to Disney World, and the awesome job I did as a father. Amazing kids.

It was a wonderful trip and a much needed reprieve, but I wished I could have done one more thing there, which would have to wait a little longer.

As I planned my proposal to Becky, a new anxiety arose within me. I knew I wanted to marry her, but buying an engagement ring triggered a strong emotional response. Doubts about our relationship overwhelmed me, and I couldn't enjoy my time with her as much. Becky gave me the space I needed, and after enough self-reflection, I realized I was afraid of losing another spouse. What if I had to do all of this again, what if the boys had to lose another mother figure?

I had to accept that we don't control death. We can try to be safe, eat well, and take care of ourselves, but it often means nothing. Healthy people get sick and die all the time. We don't know what's going to happen in the future. It all came down to this: If I could go back and tell myself at age twenty-one that Jenn would get sick, and how difficult those two years and nine months would be, would I still do it? Was the joy I experienced in the seven good years we had together worth the two years and nine months of hell? And the answer was a resounding yes, *absolutely*. No hesitation. I hope I never have to go through anything like that again, but as long as Becky and I are happy and enjoy our lives together, it's worth the risk. Once I recognized that, I was truly ready to propose.

In early July, Kayden and I went to our last regular therapy session. Devin had told me toward the end of the school year he didn't want to go anymore. It wasn't worth the amount of makeup work he had to do to stay caught up in school. His therapist had informed me just before he asked. She said the boys might express a desire to quit therapy. At some point it might just be a reminder of their loss, and actually prevent them from moving on. She advised me to allow the boys to stop when they were ready. Devin crossed that finish line in May or June.

Both Kayden and I received a clean bill of mental health that day. It felt like an accomplishment, to get the green light from my therapist to go out and live, confident in my own judgment and self-guidance. Twice in my life, therapy had been a positive, life-changing experience. I am so grateful to Misty and her assistant, Hailey. Misty steered me through the darkest, most difficult and challenging time in my life, and I will always be grateful to have had her as my therapist. I plan on going a few times a year to check in, as "maintenance", if you will, but otherwise, I'm done with therapy, and I'm all the better for it.

I proposed to Becky in late July, in San Antonio. I wanted to do something romantic, but I couldn't think of anything. I wished I could have popped the question at Disney, which seemed more romantic, but she wasn't ready at the time. I carried the ring on me the entire week in San Antonio. My therapist had advised me that proposing didn't have to be about trying to create a special moment, but that it could arise naturally. I decided to go that route. I proposed when we were feeling jubilant by being in each other's presence. It still took her by surprise. Becky is a fairly private person, and a huge public display might have made her uncomfortable. It was perfect in its own way. She said yes, and we both cried tears of joy.

Becky finished up her teacher certification requirements over the summer and found a job relatively close to me. It's still an hour drive from my house, but that's a lot better than before. Close enough to move her into our house. She spends most nights here, except for when the job requires her to be at a band or color guard rehearsal in the evening. Then she'll stay with friends in town and come back after school the next day. It's worked out wonderfully.

There are people who disagree with cohabitation before marriage, and I understand that, but we're both okay with it.

I've lived with Jenn for six months before the wedding, and while even that didn't reveal some of her deep-seated issues, it was still a good test run of our compatibility.

It's been great for our mental health as well. Becky and I are much happier now that we're not separated by a few hundred miles. We enjoy spending the evenings with the boys and our nights together.

Devin and Kayden love having Becky here. They've always loved Becky, and I think they love her more now, but they're waiting to fully give themselves to her until we're married. That makes perfect sense. They want to treat her like a mom, but she's not officially their stepmom yet, so they're biding their time. They are definitely excited about a future with Becky as their new mom. Even though I managed to figure out the "mom hug," there's something different about receiving love and affection from a woman. The boys had been missing out on that, and now they don't have to anymore.

Becky is happy, too, except for her job. Her first teaching job has proven to be an impossible task. Let's just say it's a real-life situation you would think only happens in movies. Kids who can't behave at the regular schools are sent to her school, which doesn't have enough textbooks for the students, or even enough desks for all of them to sit at. On top of that, she has to teach three to five subjects in the same class period. She's a social studies teacher, but it doesn't make any sense to teach US Government, US History Post World-War II, and Economics at the same time. That's just one example of many. There are classes where she has to juggle additional subjects with different students, and try to keep them caught up with their peers at a school getting the right kind of logistical support. On the upside, she loves teaching Color Guard. Overall, the job stresses her out, but at least her home life is happy.

My enthusiasm and passion for teaching music have returned. I'm fired up for teaching band for the first time since before Jenn had cancer. Misty and Jenn predicted this would happen, and I didn't believe either of them. The fog of depression obstructed my vision of the future. I'm so glad they were right though. I'm having fun and putting more effort into my program this year. The results have been astounding. This year's students started further behind compared to last year's students, but they've progressed much faster and are currently ahead of last year's group in several key areas. Not only am I enjoying teaching again, but the kids this year seem to like band more than my students did over the past few years.

Life hasn't been perfect, but it has been moving in a positive direction. On New Year's Eve, I told people I was optimistic this would be my best year in a while. It had to be better than the previous three years, right? I went through a period of tremendous growth and healing. My dream life seems within reach. There was just one more "first" we had to get through – the anniversary of Jenn's death.

Epilogue

Death Anniversary

"They that love beyond the world cannot be separated by it. Death cannot kill what never dies."

– WILLIAM PENN

AS THE ONE year anniversary of Jenn's death approached, our anxieties rose. It made sense that, while writing this book, my sadness would return. It did. But Cindy, Becky and Kayden were also feeling sad more often. We were thinking about Jenn and missing her more than we had been recently.

I asked around the widow/widower communities for ideas on what to do on the anniversary of a spouse's death. My plan was to take the day off work. Although I felt like I was in a good place, grief can be sneaky, and if I was going to break down, I wanted to be in a safe place. But what about the boys?

I had been hoping to send them to school and treat it like any other day, until one night, while tucking Kayden into bed. "Hey Dad, do you know it's almost December first?" he asked with a heavy voice.

"Yeah, I sure do, buddy." I responded.

"That means it's almost been a year since Mom died." He paused, then said, "I think I'm going to be sad that day. I might even cry at school that day."

I nodded and reassured, "And that's okay. It's okay to cry about missing your mom." I've had to explain the difference between crying and whining a lot, and how crying over mom is always okay as opposed to whining about me saying no to a request. "I think we're all going to cry that day, and that's alright."

After that conversation, I knew it wasn't going to be an ordinary day for the boys. I decided to keep them home from school and plan activities to help us remember Jenn, grieve, and then have fun.

I woke up at seven in the morning on the first of December, and jumped out of bed. I let everyone else sleep in. I wanted to do something special for breakfast, but didn't feel like cooking. Instead, I went to the local donut shop. The boys love donuts, so I got their favorites and left them out on the counter.

Around ten I moved Jenn's shrine from the display shelves to the dining room table. I had told everyone the day before we would sit around the table and share memories. The shrine consists of her urn, a tiny urn she had left for Becky, a picture of our family and a few decorative items.

As I set everything out, I got the sense that nobody really wanted to do this. The boys seemed happier to stay in the living room watching cartoons. Becky was still in bed, and already weeping after seeing some posts about Jenn on Facebook. I felt uncomfortable, too, but believed it was necessary. Part of moving on is to focus on the present. You can't move forward if you're stuck in a past that doesn't exist anymore. Yet it's also important to remember and acknowledge your loss, otherwise it will find a way to attack you when you least suspect it.

Around eleven I tried to gather everyone at the table. Becky was too emotional to get out of bed. I stood by her side, holding her while she was crying. I told her I was sorry that Jenn wasn't here, and reassured her she didn't have to join us at the table.

I sat with the boys in the dining room and we shared memories. Kayden was eager to share one after another. It was as if he'd been holding all of these thoughts and emotions in, waiting for this opportunity, and now they were all pouring out at once. I had to make him pause so we could take turns. It took Devin a few rounds to warm up, but then he surprised me. Devin laughed and smiled as he told his stories. A long time ago, I told him there would be a day when he would think of mom, and it would bring him happiness rather than sadness. Here I had been worried that Devin was pushing his emotions down rather than dealing with them, but he was the most okay of all of us. He and Jenn had had a special bond. Jenn had been his go-to person when he needed to talk. What a relief it was to see him reminiscing and feeling good.

Afterward, we drove to San Angelo and ate with Cindy and Charles at one of Jenn's favorite restaurants. I didn't mention to the boys why I had chosen that place, but I'm sure it was meaningful to the other adults. Everyone seemed to be in good spirits.

Next we went to a local park to release balloons. Cindy had to stop by a store to pick up her balloon order, so we spent the extra time on the playground. The boys went nuts and played for over half an hour. I was grateful they had the chance to be active on a day like this. Physical activity is therapeutic. I overheard Kayden telling another boy that it was the one year anniversary of his mom's death. What a sad conversation for a child to have.

Then we wrote messages on our balloons. Like the first time, I felt strange writing it. The idea is that the balloons float up to Heaven, where your loved one can read them. Since I don't believe in an afterlife, I don't think Jenn will ever receive another message from me. I participated regardless, focusing on writing to the Jenn that lives in my heart. My note said we were doing okay, that I hoped she thought I was doing a good job, that she was proud of us, and that she was at peace. Kayden wrote on multiple balloons. He had written about his mom's death a lot that week, and he was determined to send every last one of his thoughts and emotions to her.

It was time to release the balloons. We walked over to a clearing, counted down, and let go. The balloon ceremony is about letting go of your loss, so you can move forward. But letting go is difficult. At that moment, we all felt the sting of not being able to talk to Jenn in person.

Cindy was the first to break down. I was next to Devin, and he was okay, but Kayden was standing off to the side by himself. I saw his face starting to change, and knew his breakdown was imminent. I rushed over to him. He was looking away from me, so I kneeled and wrapped my arms around him from behind. The moment Kayden felt my embrace, he began to weep intensely. He turned around, wrapped his arms around me, and cried on my shoulder. I couldn't handle it. It is so unfair that my sons will never have their mom back. I fell apart and began to weep along with him.

Devin and I consoling Kayden through his breakdown after the balloon release.

I wasn't present enough at that point to notice who else had broken down, but what I do know is that everyone came together to console one another. Devin was one of the strongest ones among us. He went around hugging everyone to help them feel better. It was a collective mourning that had to happen. It lasted for perhaps two minutes. After we let it out, everyone's emotions settled, and then things got back to normal again.

That's how grief works. It just has to happen. You allow yourself to endure the pain, you let it do its thing, and then you get to return to life. Soon the boys were back on the playground while the adults were talking. We weren't discussing Jenn at that point, but rather the mundane events of life.

We had survived our first year without Jenn. In my depression, life without her had been my greatest fear and the largest source of my anxiety and grief. Those two years and nine months of hell were by far the darkest period of my life. It happened, but now it's over. Sometimes I still miss Jenn. Just as Angel, my first grief mentor, told me, no matter how happy I am with my life now, there will always be moments where I think, "What if she was still here?" It would be amazing if I could have her back, and more amazing if the boys could have their mom back. Becky would love to have her best friend again. But here we are, one year after her death. Life is not what we imagined it would be before cancer, but we're okay.

We're actually better than okay. Despite the occasional episodes of grief, there is a lot of joy in our lives. The boys are happy. We play together and enjoy our time as a family. Becky has added so much to our lives. We are engaged and on our way to having a "whole" family again. A sense of normalcy has returned. Once in a while, someone has a moment of missing Jenn, and we break down. It lasts a minute or two, but then we come back to the now and everything is okay.

One evening I was meditating in the bath, and realized that just being alive is good. Some may disagree with this, but not believing in an afterlife, I think to exist is far better than to not exist at all. Life is good. Just to be alive, without anything else, is good. But we are doing more than just living. We love each other. We are well, and we are happy again. It will never be the same. It's different now, but it's still good. It's just good in a different way. It's good in a new way, and it turns out that's not a bad thing.

Please listen, and believe me when I say, everything is going to be okay. You may have to lean on people for help. You may have to get therapy, start antidepressants or other medications. You may have to reach out and build a support network around you, but everything will be okay. Whatever you do, don't try to go it alone. Otherwise, you just might be stuck in that place forever. Or at least for a lot longer than you need to. But you'll be okay.

My family's cancer journey has shown me how many truly incredible people there are in the world. Due to political and religious divides, people often act hateful toward each other. But I've learned that deep down, most are kind and compassionate, willing to help in any way they can. The love and support given to us restored my faith in humanity.

That said, keep your expectations low. If you expect nothing, you can't be disappointed. You will lose plenty of "friends" along the way. Be advised that even some of the people who have really been there for you during the journey won't stick around for long after the death occurs. Jenn's friends had planned to help me go through her closet and dresser, and that, among other things, never happened. I don't hold it against them, though. They had to heal, too, and get on with their lives. Be grateful for whatever help you are offered, and accept it. Don't demand too much from yourself or others.

An important lesson I learned is that we are not entitled to anything. No matter how hard or how long you work on building your dream, it can all change in an instant. It's not fair, but such is life. Being angry about it, though it may be a necessary step in the grieving process, seems like a waste of precious time. Is it worth staying angry or depressed when your life could end at any moment? What can you do anyway?

Cherish your loved ones while you can. Before losing Jenn, I had lost my grandfather, but I wasn't as close to him in adulthood as I had been as a kid. That meant Jenn was the first traumatic loss I've experienced. The idea of growing old with Becky or that I'll get to keep my family and friends until I'm old and grey, is forever ruined. In a way that's for the best though, because I value them even more now. I'm grateful for every minute I get to spend with them, and try to enjoy it more. I hug and kiss my kids all the time. Because if anything ever happens to me, or them, I want them to know beyond the shadow of a doubt how much I loved them. People, not possessions or your job, are what's most important.

Life is far too short as it is, even if I live to be in my nineties. I don't ever want to die. Tomorrow is not guaranteed. I should be making the most I can out of every day. Every interaction with my kids matters. How I spend my time, whether or not it's doing something that will enrich my life, it matters. My work matters.

We should do everything as big as we can and to the best of our abilities. If we only get one life, it should be epic. And that life could be a lot shorter than we'd like to think, so we'd better get on with living sooner rather than later. Don't pass up the chance to be happy and do some good in the world. If you can't do the fun stuff right now, start planning for it so you can do it soon. Do great work and have fun. Love and be loved.

It's okay to move on. It is not a betrayal, and it's what your late spouse or loved one would want. Life is for the living. We must carry on.

I sincerely hope this book helped you in some way. Thank you so much for reading it, and for all your support. If you ever want to reach out to me, if you need someone to vent to, or if you have questions about anything I said in the book, my social media information is just a page flip away. Until then, thank you, and may you be happy and well.

THE END

Acknowledgements

My biggest thanks go to my late wife, Jenny Cooper, who nagged me for months to share my side of our cancer journey with the world.

Thank you to my fiancé, Rebecca Henry, who encouraged me in the writing process, and helped me remember many of the details clouded by my brain's self-defense mechanisms.

A very special thanks to my editor, Conny Shaffer, who has been such a tremendous help and resource.

Thank you to Alex Shaffer for his tireless work in formatting the book throughout the entire process.

Thank you to Savanna Bollinger, for her amazing chapter title page illustrations.

Thank you to Bayside, Eric Whitacre, Twelve Foot Ninja, and Portraits by Colleen for permission to use certain photographs.

My sincerest thanks to everyone who donated to this book's development, listed alphabetically: Chris B., Jaine C., Jami C., Larry D., BJ F., Jeannette H., Angela I., Stephanie J., Rossya K., Amy M., Katelin M., Patrick R., Gianna S., Jennifer S., Mandy S., Brian T., Lorie T., Mary U., Gene W., Shelley W., and Trish L.

Thank you to my beta readers: Kat C., Tammi M., Rhiannon, Alex S., Andrew V., M.L. V. and Patricia W.

A huge thank you to my Coffee With Coop followers, many of whom inspired me to write this book.

My thanks and love to my parents, Leslee Williams and Charles Cooper, for raising me to have good character.

Without all of your love, help and support, I would have never started this book, much less finished it. I sincerely hope you enjoyed it!

Resources

If you're interested in some of the resources I mentioned in the book, you can find more information at the following links:

Laura Bush Institute for Women's Health
www.laurabushinstitute.org

METAvivor
www.metavivor.org

Death With Dignity
www.deathwithdignity.org

Compassion & Choices
www.compassionandchoices.org

Ally's Wish
www.allyswish.org

Camp Kesem
www.campkesem.org

LNWW Late Night Widows & Widowers
https://goo.gl/6uNzNb

One Last Thing

If you enjoyed this book, I would like to ask you for a small favor. Would you please find the book on amazon.com or whichever online store you see it in, and leave an honest review? Even if you didn't like the book, that's fine. Writing a review would be a tremendous help for an unknown, independent author such as myself. Let me say thank you in advance.

Finally, if you did like this book, and are interested in following my family as we continue our life after Jenn, I would like to invite you to reach out to me at *Coffee With Coop* on any of these platforms:

Website   www.coffeewithcoop.com

Facebook   www.facebook.com/CoffeeWithCoop

YouTube   https://goo.gl/Jgd3n9

Twitter   @CoffeeWithCoop

Once again, thank you so much for reading. May you be happy and well, my friend.

About the Author

Chris Cooper, a proud father of two sons and a middle school band director, lost his wife of over nine years to a highly aggressive form of metastatic breast cancer in December of 2016. Several months before her death, he started the Facebook page Coffee With Coop as a means to share a caregiver's perspective, and in hopes of helping others cope with their own grieving process. Coffee With Coop has attracted a growing audience of over 1,700 followers, and received praise from his social media patrons for the openness, honesty and rawness of his writing.

Made in the USA
Coppell, TX
08 December 2019